Reasoning and the Explanation of Actions

Reasoning and the Explanation of Actions

DAVID MILLIGAN
Lecturer in Philosophy, University of Bristol

HARVESTER PRESS · SUSSEX
HUMANITIES PRESS · NEW JERSEY

First published in Great Britain in 1980 by
THE HARVESTER PRESS LIMITED
Publishers: John Spiers and Margaret A. Boden
16 Ship Street, Brighton, Sussex

and in the USA by
HUMANITIES PRESS INC.,
Atlantic Highlands, New Jersey 07716

© David Milligan, 1980

British Library Cataloguing in Publication Data
Milligan, David
   Reasoning and the explanation of actions. —
  (Harvester studies in philosophy).
   1. Reasoning
   2. Act (Philosophy)
   I. Title
   160   BC177
  ISBN 0-85527-433-6

Humanities Press Inc.
ISBN 0-391-01802-7

Photoset in Great Britain by
Rowland Phototypesetting Limited, Bury St Edmunds, Suffolk
Printed in the United States of America

All rights reserved

Contents

Preface		ix
I	Introduction	1
II	The Humean Conception of Deliberation	11
	I An outline of the Humean conception	11
	II An example of deliberation	13
	III Five criticisms of the Humean view	14
	IV The Humean account of factual reasoning	17
III	Wants and Desires	22
	I What are wants and desires?	22
	II The notion of a feature-want	24
	III Feature-wants relate to the future, have objects and involve pro-attitudes	26
	IV Feature-wants as action-guiding	31
IV	Are All Feature-wants Humean-desires?	34
	I The conditions for Humean-desires	34
	II The case of Matthew Dyer	36
	III Do feature-wants involve an introspectible feeling?	38
	IV Feature-wants and causality	41
	V Assumptions behind the Humean view of feature-wants	43
V	Practical Reasoning	47
	I The problem	47
	II The different contrasts for decision-making	48
	III The practice of deliberating and suppressed premisses	56
	IV Does deduction provide the standard for a good argument?	58
	V The possibility of criticism and choice	63
	VI Complexity and conflicts	65
	VII Possible defences of deductivism	69

VI	An Alternative Account of Deliberation	73
	I Good reasons justify	73
	II Comparisons	76
	III Evaluative comparisons	82
	IV Decision-making	89
	V The process of deliberation	91
VII	Action	94
	I Deliberation and feature-wants	94
	II Closing the gap between reasoning and action	97
VIII	Explaining by Reasons	105
	I Reasons and feature-wants	105
	II Reasons are evaluations	107
	III Reasons and rules	114
IX	Reasons and the Logical Connection Argument	123
	I Melden's version of the argument	123
	II What-and why-explanations	125
	III Must reasons be internal to actions?	128
	IV Evaluation and the connection between reasons and actions	131
X	Are Reasons Causes?	133
	I The origination of voluntary and involuntary actions	133
	II Are evaluations the causes of actions?	138
	III The evaluation of reasons and the possibility of an infinite regress	139
	IV Reasons are not causes	141
XI	Non-deliberative actions	143
	I Different types of non-deliberative actions	143
	II Immediate actions	145
	III Habitual actions	148
	IV Unconscious reasons	153
XII	Compatibility	159
	I Actions and bodily movements	159
	II The compatibility of causal explanations of actions with explanations by reasons	165
	III Explanations and responsibility	167

XIII Verifiability	171
I Verification and covering-laws	171
II Verification and evaluations	174
III Verification and responsibility	176
XIV Conclusion	178
Notes	183
Summary of Examples	188
Index	191

Preface

> If there be any in this assembly, any dear
> friend of Caesar's, to him I say that Brutus'
> love to Caesar was no less than his. If then that
> friend demand why Brutus rose against
> Caesar, this is my answer: Not that I
> lov'd Caesar less, but that I lov'd Rome more.
> Had you rather Caesar were living, and die
> all slaves, than that Caesar were dead, to
> live all free men?
>
> (*Julius Caesar*, Act III, Scene ii)

So Brutus explains his part in the murder of Caesar to the Roman citizens. He gives a reason for what he did: he loved Rome more than he loved Caesar. Assuming that Brutus is not deceiving himself or others, how does his reason explain his action? What is the relation of his greater love for Rome to his action in murdering Caesar? Is it a causal relation? Or is there a contradiction in supposing that the reason Brutus gives could have caused his action? How is this kind of explanation related to other types of explanation—physiological, psychological or sociological?

These questions indicate the topics with which I shall be concerned in this book, but my main attention is directed towards reasons and the way they explain; until we are clear about them, the other questions cannot be tackled. My approach is less direct than may be usual. I do not start with how reasons are related to the actions they explain—how, for example, Brutus' love for Rome is related to his murder of Caesar. Rather I start by examining the ways in which agents, such as Brutus, deliberate and come to conclusions about what to do. If their actions are deliberative, then the process of thought by which they decide what to do plays an essential part in the origination of their actions. In his deliberation Brutus decides that his love for Rome is more important than his love for Caesar, and thus forms a reason for his action. It is through his evaluation of the different wants and interests he has that he finds an answer to what he should do.

A discussion of the structure of deliberation is essential to my argument. I reject any view of it which takes reasoning to be no more than deductive or causal reasoning. Rather, I see it as a matter of weighing up reasons for and against different conclusions and deciding which one is best supported. It is through his evaluation of the relevant factors that an agent determines what is to be a reason, a good reason, and finally a decisive reason. When Brutus murders Caesar as a result of his deliberation, he has considered various factors and assessed their relative importance. In deciding that the welfare of Rome outweighs all other factors, he decides that it is a sufficient reason to determine his action. His desire for the welfare of Rome is not in itself sufficient to result in his action. It is only through his evaluation of it that it becomes so. This point is fundamental to an account of reasons and throws doubts on at least some causalist accounts of them.

My methods may seem unorthodox because they deliberately avoid the fashionable reliance on the techniques and concepts of formal and philosophical logic. Valuable insights may result from using those techniques, but I believe their excessive use can blind the eye to elements in experience which cannot be framed in their terms. I prefer to look at particular examples and use an approach which involves a careful examination of the ways people feel, think and act.

Two influences do not get the acknowledgement they deserve in the text, because my debts to them are so extensive and pervasive. Roy Edgley's *Reason in Theory and Practice*[1] raises fundamental questions in an exciting and illuminating way. I do not agree with all he says, and there is much that I say which I am sure he would reject. Yet any reader of that book and this will be in no doubt that I owe much to it; I am also indebted to him for his detailed discussion of the paper[2] in which I started to formulate my views on reasons.

Preface

My debt to John Macmurray[3] is great. I was lucky enough to be taught by him and to be briefly a colleague of his though I did not always recognise my good fortune. Through the years I have come to realise how important his approach is and how much I and many others have to learn from him. His views and the style in which they are presented are unfashionable and much neglected in academic philosophy, though less so outside. His working-out of the consequences of the primacy of action draws attention to many of the insights since developed in philosophy of action and results in a coherent and wide-ranging philosophical view of both depth and humanity. Because his ideas lie so far outside the main trend in recent philosophy, they are difficult to absorb, and I do not think that what I say does as much justice to his ideas as it should.

I should like to express my thanks to my colleagues in Bristol for all their help and to two in particular. Stephan Körner has given much encouragement and help over a number of years. David Hirschmann read through a late draft of the book and with his customary consideration and acuity made detailed comments without which the arguments would have been more obscure and more flawed.

I should also like to thank Margaret Boden for the interest she has shown, the care with which she read a draft and the comments without the benefit of which my argument would have been much weaker.

Those who type a book engage in a rather onerous technical exercise, for which much thanks is owing. On this occasion Doreen Harding and, especially, Yvonne Kaye did far more than this, by the interest they took in the whole enterprise, by their great competence, by never refusing any demand however unreasonable and finally by always being kind and helpful far beyond the call of duty.

Lastly, my thanks go to my children, Robert and Ruth, for accepting the puzzlement of having a philosopher for a father and, above all, to my wife.

I
Introduction

Explaining actions is both an everyday activity and the purpose of much empirical enquiry. The resulting explanations show great variety in style and structure; there may be conflict not only about which explanation is correct, but also about which type of explanation is appropriate. The latter conflict immediately gives rise to philosophical problems about the nature and status of the various types of explanation and about the relation of different explanations of the same action to each other. These problems are not remote from the practice of explaining, and without answers to them the explanations, and what is implied by them will be unclear. A psychiatrist gives an explanation for the action of a criminal. How far and in what way is the criminal's responsibility for his action affected by the action being explainable in such a way? Do different types of explanation affect it differently? Again a sociologist explains a poor performance in standard tests by children in a certain school in terms of their social environment. What are the consequences of accepting such an explanation? The answer depends on what status such explanations are alleged to have and the nature of the link between social environment and educational success which is thereby implied.

Consider another example: non-accidental injuries to children by their parents. The professionals often explain these assaults in terms of various features of the parents' early life, such as he or she having been similarly assaulted while a child; they may also bring into the explanation the social and physical environment in which the parents live. Such explanations suggest that an assault is the result of these factors and that therefore the parent is not responsible, or at least not wholly responsible for his action. Thus these individuals ought not to be punished, but rather should be given treatment and help. At the other extreme is the layman who is enraged by such attempts to excuse someone who in his judgment has done something wicked; the culprits deserve to be and must be punished. He sees the parent as not having exercised the required control over his actions, a control he should be perfectly capable of exercising.

It may be that in a particular case the layman is wrong. But even if the emotive tone of some such reactions is rejected there is nevertheless often some truth in what is being said. The element of truth does not, however, necessarily imply that the professionals are wrong, but only that what follows from their explanations has been misunderstood—most of all by the layman. Can we not explain, sympathise and help even in a case where someone has acted wrongly and could have acted otherwise? Is it not possible that factors from someone's early life explain his action and that at the same time he has some kind of choice in the way he acts? Though one may feel intuitively certain that such a position of reconciliation is possible, and in many cases correct, it is still difficult to make sense of it. To find an account of explanation which shows exactly what is happening when an explanation is given, and which relates explanations to the possibility of choice and responsibility, is essential if we are to be able to understand the action of the parent in assaulting his child and the relation to his action of his past, his present situation and how he sees that situation. Above all it is essential if the right decision is to be reached about how the parent should be treated.

In order to reconcile explanations of the kind mentioned with choice and responsibility, it is not enough to show that the agent can at the same time be influenced by factors over which he has no control and be responsible; it is also necessary to understand the way he exercises a choice which is not arbitrary, to understand how he acts for a reason and how explanations in terms of external factors can be reconciled with explanations in terms of reasons. Indeed an understanding of the way an agent comes to have a reason and the way such reasons explain is a precondition for achieving the required reconciliation. This study of reasons is directed towards providing such an understanding.

The problem of reconciliation is not the only one to which such a study should be relevant. There are questions about understanding oneself and others, the answers to which have implications for ways of giving help and advice. There are questions related to the concepts of a person and an agent and hence the connections between a study of reasons and ethics are important. There are questions related to the nature of decisions, answers to which are relevant to theories about decision-making, whether descriptive or normative. I shall not be able to discuss the implications of what I have to say in these areas; but I do believe that one of the most important tests of any account, such as mine, is whether or not it serves to increase our understanding of explanations of all sorts and of the actions which are being explained, both in everyday contexts and in the more specialised ones just mentioned. Even at times when the discussion may have to be abstract and academic, its relevance to such diverse problems as the non-accidental injury of children and decision-making in industry or in government must never be lost sight of.

The problems about the nature of reasons are usually discussed in terms of whether reasons are causes and whether explanation by means of reasons is a form of causal explanation. So much has been written that it might be thought that nothing more can usefully be said; however, many accounts of reasons are unsatisfactory, both in what they say about reasons and in the way they relate reasons to other kinds of explanation of action. To approach the question directly may be stultifying, but a less direct approach may be more productive. Thus an account of whether reasons are causes may be more successful if it is approached by way of considering how an agent comes to have a reason, and what part reasons play in the origination of actions and the making of decisions. Reasons are not mere abstractions which have logical relations; we cannot understand them by analysing the logical relation of reason-statements to action-descriptions. To separate them from the context in which they occur as part of the agent's thinking, or from the process by which he settles on the way he is going to act, is dangerous. Too often reasons are seen simply in relation to the action they explain without considering what could have led up to the action and without looking at the way in which the action actually originated. I shall, therefore, examine the process by which agents come to act, claiming that an explanation by means of the agent's reasons is essentially about how he came to act in the way he did. To understand what is meant by an explanation we have to understand the relation between what is mentioned in the explanation and the various elements which played a part in the action coming about. I shall therefore give an account of the origination of actions.

For the purposes of my discussion I shall not question the legitimacy of any explanations. Some of them are correct, others may be incorrect. But which are correct cannot be decided *a priori*. Tempting though it may be to do so, it is a mistake to rule out as illegitimate all explanations of a particular type on philosophical grounds alone.[1] Not only do I accept that everyday explanations can explain, but also that sociological and psychological enquiry can provide correct explanations, even of the same actions to which everyday explanations are given. I shall try to show that these different explanations in spite of contrary appearances are compatible with each other, as they must also be with physiological explanations of the bodily movements required for the action.

I shall also assume that free-will, choice and responsibility are conceivable and so cannot be ruled out on logical or conceptual grounds. These concepts are notoriously controversial and might seem to need definition. I shall not attempt this. Rather I shall accept these concepts in the form they take in their everyday use. My account of the way actions originate will, I hope, throw some light on them and what lies behind them, and remove the apparent threat which an explanation makes to the action explained being free. I am not claiming that all or any actions are free; that is not an issue here. It cannot be settled *a priori*. Rather anything that is said about explanation must leave open the question of whether any particular action is free. Certain types of explanation may require that an action is or is not free, but which type of explanation is appropriate to which actions must be left to an examination of each action.

The dispute about whether explanations by reasons and explanations by causes are exclusive or whether the former make up a sub-class of the latter is not one in which I shall take sides, since I am far from clear what I would be committing myself to in joining either. Partly this is because it is not always clear what concept of causality is being used. I do not intend to discuss causality as such and so, rather than trying to settle the issue of whether reasons are causes, I shall try to distinguish different kinds of explanations of action and see what each consists of. My chief interest is in reasons as they explain and in the reasoning by which agents come to a decision about what to do. Indeed what I have to say is almost as much a view of reasoning as it is a view of explanation. I shall ask: What is it for an agent to have a reason? How is the reason for an action arrived at? In the case of deliberative actions, how does the agent arrive at his reasons? What process of reasoning must he go through in order to form his reasons? What are the implications of an action having an explanation in terms of reasons?

To talk of reasons immediately suggests ideas of rationality, of having good reasons and of being reasonable, and this leads to questions of justification. Though I cannot avoid mentioning justification it is not my primary concern. It is the reasons upon which the agent acts that are important, whether they are good or bad. Our assessment of the way an agent comes to his decision does not affect the nature or the correctness of the explanation. Of course there is a connection between explanation and justification. When an agent comes to a decision to act, he believes that from the point of view he then takes his decision is justified. To reason about what to do and to act from reasons is to believe at the time of acting that they are good reasons. However, looking for the explanation of an action is different from looking for its justification, though it may well involve trying to discover what justified the action to the agent at the time he acted.

The association of giving reasons with justification often

leads to a view of reasons as essentially connected with logic and deduction, and the belief that there are therefore indubitable tests of what is rational. That view is one I do not share. Reasons are essentially evaluative,[2] and in some cases —but not in all—the principles of evaluation are principles of logic. Not all reasons are deductive and this is especially true in the context of actions, where to decide that a factor is a good reason is to evaluate that factor.

This view of reasons comes much more to the fore in an examination of the way deliberative actions originate. In order to understand the explanation of such actions we have to look at the processes of thought by which an agent finally decides on his action. The explanation of why the action takes place must be in terms of how the agent comes to make up his mind, and that will depend on the way he thinks about and assesses his situation and the courses of action he believes are open to him. The agent's reason must similarly depend on what he thinks and the factor mentioned in his reason is something which he has taken account of in his deliberation; indeed it is that factor which, as he deliberates, swings him decisively behind the line of action he takes.

To see what a reason is, how it explains an action and how it relates to the action it explains, it is therefore essential to ascertain what makes a factor about which the agent deliberates into a reason for his action. This is the key to my approach. Though reasons can be and are given for immediate actions, for the most part I shall confine my attention to deliberative actions. I believe that it is from this type of action that the notion of a reason derives its sense, and the way in which reasons explain other types of action depends on the way reasons are used in the context of deliberative actions.

My account is divided into three main parts. In the first I shall discuss the nature of deliberation. In the second I shall apply the conclusions reached about deliberation to reach a view about the explanation of deliberative actions by means of reasons. In the final part I shall consider how this view can be extended to other types of action, and also how it can deal with certain other problems about the explanation of actions.

Introduction

The view of deliberation which I present in the first part is rather different from that which is generally assumed or implied by most accounts of reasoning and explanation. In order to develop it I shall make a contrast with what I call the Humean view of deliberation, according to which deliberation can only consist of deductive and causal reasoning. The causal reasoning establishes the facts required for the agent to be able to infer from his wants that the action in question is the one to be done. I do not argue that anyone has actually held the Humean view, though it seems to me that something like it, perhaps in a less extreme form, is assumed or implied by what Hume says and indeed still seems to be assumed in much contemporary writing about explanation. What is wrong with this view lies partly in its account of the wants and desires which form the basic motivation towards action and partly in the account of reasoning it presupposes.

I shall discuss both of these flaws. The Humean view of wants requires that wants can only be the result of thought if they are derived from other wants which are not the result of thought but are immediate, and thus are like impulses which rise up in the agent uninvited and unguided. They are— Hume suggests—impressions, things which happen to an agent and which he can observe in himself. Undoubtedly some wants, which I shall call impulse-desires, fit this description in most respects. If, however, a concept of a want is required such that all actions originate in a want, then there is no reason why all these wants, which I shall call feature-wants, should be impulse-desires. Some feature-wants may be determined by the agent himself and need not be caused by anything external to the agent's deliberation or volition. Equally the notion of a feature-want is not such that all feature-wants must act causally—in a narrow sense of that term—to determine actions. With some feature-wants the agent can choose whether or not to satisfy them.

I then argue against the supposition that the only kinds of reasoning which can occur in deliberation are deductive or causal. To take such a view leaves no room for choice by the agent, gives few grounds on which his reasoning can be criticised and requires that all feature-wants are impulse-desires. It leaves no way of solving conflicts between feature-wants or reasons except by supposing that the conflict is between opposing impulses or forces and that it is solved by one desire being the strongest. It also fails to do justice to the way people deliberate in ordinary situations and to the significance of that deliberation for the decisions they make.

An alternative to the Humean view of deliberation is, therefore, required. In deliberating about what to do an agent —in theory if not always in practice—has to decide which factors are relevant and has to take note of the features of his present situation, of the different actions open to him and of the consequences of those actions. Some of these factors are not such as to warrant being taken into account in considering the advantages and disadvantages of the alternatives open to him; nor are they such as to warrant forming a feature-want related to them. But many will be, and the agent then has to consider the relevant feature-wants and, in so far as they indicate different lines of action, weigh them against each other. He evaluates the feature-wants relative to each other in the particular context and reaches a conclusion. This may be attacked by suggesting that there are factors he has neglected or that factors he thought to be important are less important and vice versa. Thus reasons may be given against his conclusion, just as he may give reasons to support his conclusion. He can indicate what his feature-wants or reasons are and what his assessment of them is. The Humean would claim that any attack or defence of the agent's conclusion must either relate to the deductive reasoning he used or to the material to which he applied such reasoning; to suppose otherwise, he would continue, is to suggest that what is to count as adequate reasoning is to some extent a matter of taste. I shall argue that this is not so and that there are types of reasoning which are neither deductive nor inductive. Admittedly it may be impossible to point to objective principles of reasoning by which anyone's deliberation may be checked; admittedly it is in practice difficult to separate the agent's reasoning from the material to which the reasoning is applied: but it does not follow either that it is impossible to give an account of alternative types of reasoning or that reasoning of such types is not open to rational criticism.

In determining those factors which are relevant and those which are sufficiently important to play a part in the final decision the agent is deciding on the factors which are to constitute reasons for or against different actions. Of those reasons the ones he takes to be most important and to constitute good reasons for doing the action are what explains the action. The presence of the factors is not alone sufficient for the action to take place; it is also necessary for the agent to decide that these factors provide a reason, and moreover a sufficient reason, for doing the action. To be a reason the agent has to decide that the factor is a reason for him and this is an autonomous decision of his; he commits himself to his evaluation of the importance of the factor in deciding that it is a reason. Thus to state that a factor is the agent's reason for an action is to indicate how he evaluated that factor.

When an account of reasons and how they explain actions is given, attention is usually directed towards the content of the reason. If a reason is characterised as a desire and a belief, then the claim that the agent's reason is the cause of his action is the claim that his desire—with his belief—is the cause. However, this last claim is mistaken, since the desire cannot constitute the reason and at the same time be by itself the cause of the action. For, if the desire is to become the agent's reason, it must be evaluated in a particular way by the agent; he must decide that the desire is to constitute a reason. Is, perhaps, that evaluation or decision about the desire the cause of the action? If a cause is whatever leads to or brings about an effect, then certainly it is a cause. But if a narrower sense of 'cause' is used, the question is more difficult. For, on the one hand, the evaluation is not independent of the action, even if there is no logical connection. On the other hand, the evaluation seems to be a necessary and sufficient condition for the action taking place. I prefer to distinguish explanations by reasons from explanations by causes because it is less misleading, though in the end I do not think a great deal turns on it.

The discussion of this topic completes the main argument of the book. In the final chapters I shall do three things. Firstly, I shall extend the account of reasons to non-deliberative actions, whether they be immediate or habitual or arise from unconscious reasons. Secondly, I shall show how my account copes with the problem of the possibility of different types of explanation for the same action. I shall argue that such explanations are not only compatible, but complementary, and that therefore there is no difficulty in reconciling the possibility of explanation with the agent being responsible for the action explained. This argument has some importance for the relation of commonsense explanations to explanations in the social sciences. Thirdly, I shall briefly raise some issues about the verification of explanations by reasons, and show that we need not be tempted by problems of verifiability into thinking that these explanations must, or should, take a covering-law form.

II
The Humean Conception of Deliberation

I—An outline of the Humean conception

In Books II and III of *A Treatise of Human Nature* Hume argues against the rationalist account of reason as a source of morality and as an influencing motive of the will. While seeing reason as lacking the powers the rationalists took it to have, he nevertheless does not disagree greatly with their view of the nature of reason and the forms reasoning or deliberation can take:

> The understanding exerts itself after two different ways, as it judges from demonstration or probability; as it regards the abstract relations of our ideas, or those relations of objects, of which experience only gives us information.[1]

This suggests that deliberation is restricted to one or other of these ways in which the understanding can operate: 'the comparing of ideas and the inferring of matter of fact'.[2] The first is usually interpreted as being that which depends on the analysis of concepts or the employment of deductive reasoning; the second as reasoning about questions of fact which involves the discovery and application of causal statements based, according to Hume, on observed regularities.

This conception of deliberation—which I shall call the Humean conception—is, I think, implicit in many discussions of the explanation of action, and some of the mistakes made in those discussions are connected with the limitations of this conception. I shall therefore examine it in some detail and by criticising it develop my own account. It may be that the strong form of that conception, which I attack, has never been used, but my interest in it is to have a view for my account to be contrasted with.

Hume argues that reason must be restricted to the apparently limited activities of comparing ideas and discovering matters of fact. This seems to imply that, in coming to a decision to act, if our passions are given, we are confined to reasoning deductively about them and using causal knowledge to ascertain the means of achieving their satisfaction or the ends to which they direct us. Our passions are original existences, '. . . original facts and realities, compleat in themselves, and implying no reference to other passions, volitions, and actions'.[3] They thus do not seem to be anything arrived at by means of a process of thought. The only exception can be when a desire directed towards a given end to which reason shows the means gives rise to a desire for those means. To suggest reason can conflict with or control the passions is misleading. Apparent examples of conflict are dealt with in two ways: firstly, Hume suggests that what seems to be a reason may merely be a calm passion, not recognised because it lacks the violence of emotion mistakenly taken to be essential to a passion; secondly, when an action is described as being contrary to reason, he claims that what is meant is that the passion giving rise to the action is accompanied by some judgment which is contrary to reason. This is therefore an account of the way action must originate which at the best leaves a very restricted rôle to reason and which confines deliberation to deduction and the acquiring and applying of causal knowledge.

Another way of stating the Humean view, though it is not Hume's, is in terms of a practical syllogism, with one premiss embodying a statement of the passion, desire or end, and the other stating that a particular action will satisfy the desire or lead to the end, while the conclusion is either the action already referred to or a statement that this is the action to do. Various formulations and interpretations of the practical syllogism are given. But whatever practical syllogisms are or ought to be, they do seem to be taken as in some way giving the basic structure of our reasoning about actions. However I claim that even though the practical syllogism—in some versions at least—is an improvement on the Humean view, it remains closely connected with it and fails to provide a satisfactory account of deliberation.

II—An example of deliberation

Let me begin with a particular example of deliberation and see how the Humean would deal with it. In order to show what may happen or may be implicit in what happens in deliberation, I shall make the deliberation more complicated than the decision may seem to require. Thomas Fagg is a salesman and an habitual smoker. He is considering whether or not to give up smoking. He begins by asking about the consequences of smoking and the consequences of giving it up. He tries to assess the evidence about how far smoking is generally bad for health and in what way that evidence is applicable to his case. The statistical evidence may indicate the probability of certain consequences for people who share certain characteristics. Whether an individual has one of these characteristics may be easy to determine as, for instance, is the case with the number of cigarettes smoked; but where it is the person's state of health or the nature of their job and the stress within it, then it may be more difficult. However Thomas Fagg's conclusion is reached, he ends up with a statement about the degree of likelihood of each of the possible consequences of continuing smoking. Similarly he tries to assess the consequences of giving it up. He may be sure about the effects which giving up smoking will have on his own psychological state, but less certain about its effects on his family and friends, whether in terms of their feelings or their consequent actions. He also considers more marginal effects such as those related to the feelings of clients towards himself and his firm when he refuses a cigarette. Even though there may be a correct assessment of these consequences, it is possible—and even probable—that it never would be made.

After ascertaining the facts, Thomas Fagg then considers his wants and desires, interests and values in relation to them. He wants to be healthy and happy; to be liked by his customers and successful in selling to them; he wants to have enough money to buy a new car; he feels he ought to do what he can not to cause suffering to his wife and family by his early death. As a result of these considerations he decides to give up smoking.

According to the Humean, this deliberation must take the form of deducing a conclusion from premisses given by the facts and by his wants or desires, or, to use Hume's more general term, his passions. The passions seem to be reducible to some kind of feeling immediately given—a feeling which the smoker would observe in himself.

There are points at which this Humean account of coming to a decision is not sufficiently clear. The model for the Humean view, and indeed for a practical syllogism, is more evident in the simpler case where there is a practical problem to be solved, where for instance the engine of my car will not start. Here one premiss could be: I want my car to start. The other premiss will result from finding out why it will not start, and what will make it start. In this case the trouble may be that the lead to one of the plugs is worn. The second premiss would then be: Replacing the lead will make the engine start. The conclusion is easily derived whether in the form of a statement or an action.

We have to ask whether, in the example of the smoker, we can in fact show that a deduction can be discovered. I would argue that either such a deduction cannot be found or that any deduction which is found does not include all the elements in the deliberation. Indeed, in a typical case in which an agent has reasons for his actions, or acts on the basis of reasons, the reasons have nothing to do with deductive reasoning. It may be that in some cases the agent's decision seems to follow validly or with certainty from what he claims as reasons, or from a filled-out statement of his reasons. But this appearance is misleading, and the fact that a deduction can be constructed does not imply that the final decision could have been arrived at solely by deduction. In a typical case, like that of Thomas Fagg, the agent's reasons are not deductively related to his decision, though his decision is still justifiable or defensible.

III—*Five criticisms of the Humean view*

Let me now indicate five of the main ways in which the Humean view is open to criticism in so far as it provides an account of the thinking which is involved in coming to a practical decision. The first relates to reasoning about matters of fact. Such reasoning can be far more complicated and can include a far wider range of types of thinking than the Humean view suggests. The second criticism is of the account it gives or assumes of desires, feelings, values or passions. They are not always original existences or immediate impulses, but may themselves be the subject of thought and deliberation in a way not allowed by the Humean view. The smoker may not be sure what he wants or values, and to decide on this he does not merely observe himself or perform experiments, whether real or hypothetical, on himself. Rather he thinks about what he really wants to do and his thinking does not need to be deductive. The third criticism of the Humean view is that it bears little relation to the way people actually reason, and the attempt to reduce all deliberation to logical reasoning makes it almost trivial and in no way allows for the variety and complexity of thinking that may take place when an agent is deciding how to act. Moreover it suggests a relation between the support for the agent's conclusion about what to do and that conclusion which is too restricted.

Fourthly, it seems to me that the Humean view fails to account for cases of conflict where passions pull the person in different directions. The smoker is not simply trying to deliberate about how to achieve a fixed or agreed end. He is deliberating about different courses of action, towards each of which he is in some ways inclined and in other ways disinclined because of the extent to which they achieve different ends. He may be able to produce an argument about each of these ends, and each of these arguments may be reducible to something like a syllogism. But it is difficult to see how they are to be brought together. Consider a very simple form of such a conflict situation. Suppose Thomas Fagg is only concerned with two things, being healthy and not being irritable. These might then be two of his arguments:

    (i) Giving up smoking will lead to better health.
       I want better health.
       ∴ Give up smoking.

and (ii) Giving up smoking will make me more irritable.
I do not want to be more irritable.
∴. Do not give up smoking.

The problem is to see how all four premisses can be combined to produce one conclusion. It seems that on the Humean account we can only do so by seeing the wants as in some way forces of different strength, and thus providing an additional premiss: my wanting better health is stronger than my wanting not to be irritable. I am unhappy about the Humean view here not only because it is forced to give an inadequate account of wants but also because it leads to an inadequate account of the ways we can sort out conflicts.

My fifth and final criticism is that it is difficult to see at what point in his deliberation an agent can, according to the Humean, exercise his free-will. The only choice available to the agent, it sometimes seems, is to choose whether or not to argue validly. This is not to claim, on the one hand, that every action which results from deliberation is freely chosen. I think it is possible for an alcoholic to deliberate about how to get a drink, or about the easiest way to satisfy his compulsive desire. Nor, on the other hand, is it to claim that all choices involve deliberation. The point is that some choices require deliberation, and some deliberation involves choice, and an adequate account of deliberation must allow for these possibilities.

It might appear that my aim is to give a satisfactory account of reason in its practical context and to show that this is different from reason in its theoretical context, but this is not my intention. There is a well known division between those who see theoretical and practical reason as the application of the same kind of reason to different contexts and those who see a distinction between the practical application of theoretical reason and practical reason itself. It might seem that I am advocating a rather radical version of the latter view, since I claim that deliberation or practical reason is far more than the use of induction and deduction with which theoretical reason is usually identified. But that is not the case. I do allow that some kind of distinction may be made in a rough and ready fashion between theoretical and practical reason, either in terms of the conclusions being judgments or choices, or in terms of the subject matter being questions of fact or questions about what is to be done. Nevertheless I do not see any grounds for saying that the kinds of reasoning involved must be of a radically different type. My view is rather that the usual account of theoretical reason is inadequate and needs to be widened to include those other forms of thinking and reasoning which are required for a satisfactory account of practical reason. Thus my reaction to the Humean view of deliberation is that it involves an idea of reason that is inadequate not only in the sphere of action but also in the sphere of fact.

IV—*The Humean account of factual reasoning*

Though the sphere of fact is not my concern, it may nevertheless be useful, before looking at the other criticisms, to examine very briefly the Humean account of reasoning as applied to it. According to the Humean view, reasoning in relation to facts can only be used either to establish causal statements and laws of nature or to apply them. The former are arrived at by making inductions on the basis of observed regularities. In the latter we use generalisations either to predict what will be the consequences of certain events or, having a definite end in mind, to work out what means will lead to its accomplishment. To do this we simply make deductions from the premisses which consist of the generalisations and of observation statements. It might seem that Popper, in attacking induction as the method of science, is attacking this rather limited view of thinking. But, although much of what he says is right, his replacement of induction by the hypothetico-deductive method does not lead to any change of view about what form thinking or reasoning can take. Popper thinks that the formation of hypotheses is not a rational matter, and that once they are obtained there is no other reasoning possible but deduction and checking with observations. About the formation of hypotheses he is explicit:

> The initial stage, the act of conceiving or inventing a theory, seems to me neither to call for logical analysis nor to be susceptible of it. The question how it happens that a new idea occurs to a man . . . may be of great interest to empirical psychology; but it is irrelevant to the logical analysis of scientific knowledge. This latter is concerned not with *questions of fact* . . . but only with questions of *justification or validity* . . .[4]

Popper is right in thinking that questions of discovery are different from questions of justification, and there may be good reasons for suggesting that anything said about discovery is irrelevant to his main concern, the justification of scientific theories. But that does not require us to dismiss questions about discovery as purely psychological or only of importance to psychology. We must ask whether those of our concepts which are related to minds, thinking and action are such that sense can be made of the possibility and nature of discovery. If our concepts are such that discoveries can only result from hunches or lucky intuitions and cannot involve any rational processes then perhaps there is something wrong with these concepts. Any logical analysis of scientific method should not only be concerned with justification, but also with the processes of thought and the concepts used, with the assumptions made in all scientific activity. I would claim, indeed, that discovery and justification are not as unconnected as Popper suggests, and that we may be able to learn something about justification by understanding discovery rather better.

Why should it be thought that discovery cannot be a rational matter? The reason lies, perhaps, in the assumption that if discovery involves thought or is rational, it must use deduction, and deduction by its very nature can introduce nothing into the conclusion, into what is alleged to be discovered, that was not in the premisses from which the discoverer started. Originality and deduction seem to be exclusive. But deduction, as I shall argue in Chapter V, does not need to be the whole of what constitutes thinking, even when the thinking is leading to a conclusion. The scientist in making discoveries is just as creative as is the artist and what the latter does can be both original and an exercise of the mind. In some cases, though not necessarily in all, the creative process is intelligible though not predictable. It may be difficult to allow such a possibility so long as it is supposed that reasoning must conform to the Humean pattern. Widen the notion of reasoning, of the types of thinking possible in deliberation, and the grounds for seeing an incompatibility between creativity and reasoning may disappear.

The possibility of a form of reasoning in science other than induction and deduction has been explored by N. R. Hanson.[5] Making use of the insights of Peirce, he argues for there being a logic of discovery and for the formation of hypotheses involving a form of inference. This he calls retroduction. Typically the scientist would start with an anomaly, a fact which does not fit current theory; he then searches for a hypothesis to explain the anomaly. Any such hypothesis, though not reached by deduction or induction and thus not justified, is worth considering; that it explains the anomaly is a reason for considering it. Clearly such a view, if acceptable, would provide support for my claims. Hanson's account has been criticised by P. Alexander,[6] and his suggestion that Hanson has not shown that there is a distinct and different form of *inference* in retroduction seems to me right. But I think that Peirce and Hanson are getting at an important point, though perhaps wrongly characterising it. They seem mistakenly to want to preserve a strong analogy between the reasoning involved in discovery and deduction. I doubt if 'inference' in its usually understood sense is the right word to describe the former reasoning. Nor am I happy with the suggestion that there is one single logic of discovery. My claim is that reasoning is involved in discovery, that some types of that reasoning have been indicated by Peirce and Hanson, but that there will be others involved as well.

So far in considering the Humean account of factual thinking I have only mentioned the thinking involved in science. What about the thinking of an agent who is trying to establish the facts of a situation in which he has to decide how to act? There are various aspects of this situation which he will have to consider. The agent will have to ascertain exactly what situation he is in and pure observation, if there is such a thing, will rarely be enough; he may need to discover how to achieve a desired end and also to discover as far as possible the consequences of each of the actions open to him. In so far as these processes involve the application of already established knowledge it may seem that difficulties would be unlikely. However, such an application may not be straight-forward. Consider the case of George Green trying to decide whether or not to plant out his tomatoes. The consequences of the decision may not be of great moment, but the difficulties are typical of more important cases. Here we are only concerned with how he decides what will be the consequences of either planting out or not planting out his tomatoes. He may be able to consult horticultural textbooks, but they are unlikely to be able to deal with all the particular circumstances. George will have to decide what factors are relevant—the weather, the chemical composition of the soil, the site he has chosen, his absences from home at work or on holiday and so on. Next he has to consider how each of the factors will affect his tomatoes according to whether or not they are planted out. Lastly he has to try and combine all this information together. It is not clear how the deductive model could give an account of the reasoning here. It is plain that in practice George Green would not make a deduction and that nevertheless he does reason. If decisions of this type were to be made on a large scale, then rules might be devised, information coded and a computer used to produce a decision. But the fact that decisions can be made in this way does not mean they must be or that they are best made thus.

Consequences involve not only changes in the material world. All actions have at least some effect on the agent, even if it is only that he is aware of having acted, and in most cases they have an effect on other agents. Much of the time no thought may be given to this aspect of the consequences, but sometimes it is important. In considering the effects, the agent may limit himself to what he and others feel, but he may also have to predict what actions others will take as a result of what he does. Though his estimations of all these reactions may be sound, they are rarely based on the straightforward application of established generalisations. The status of such generalisations as have been formulated is far from clear and their automatic application is not likely to result in correct predictions. But again I can see no reason for suggesting that such estimations do not involve thought on the part of the agent.

These remarks are not sufficient to justify my suggestion that the Humean view is inadequate even for thinking about matters of fact. To consider the matter further would take me far from my main argument. However what has been said may indicate that the Humean view at least requires defence at this point.

III
Wants and Desires

I—*What are wants and desires?*

Hume claimed that actions can never originate in reason, but only in the passions. A contemporary Humean would be more likely to express this in terms of wants and desires: all actions are caused by wants or desires and having a desire is assumed to be something which happens to an agent, like an impulse or force acting on him so that it is the strongest desire which determines the action. Accordingly, there are only two functions of deliberation: to ascertain the facts of a situation in which an agent is called on to act so that his desires respond to the situation as it really is, and to discover the means by which an agent can satisfy his wants or desires.

The account of desires is one of the weaknesses of the Humean view of deliberation. One criticism of that view relates to its assumption that a desire or a want must be or must involve something which occurs in the consciousness of the agent. However we can and do attribute a desire to an agent without its being necessary for him to have any knowledge of whether he had such thoughts or feelings. An agent can desire something and can act in order to satisfy that desire without there being any corresponding conscious event.[1]

My criticisms are different. The view is inadequate not because it takes desires to involve a conscious state or event, but on the contrary because only one kind of such states or events is allowed for. I do not deny that there are cases of desires which do not involve a conscious event and that the Humean view fails to take account of them. But unless there are cases of desires to which some conscious events are integral, I suggest we can have no adequate understanding of desires. As with so many psychological concepts which are applicable whether or not there is a relevant conscious event, it is the cases where the conscious event is present which are central; without the existence of these cases such concepts would be unintelligible. Thus while the Humean view is inadequate in not allowing for the possibility of non-central cases, far more important is its failure to allow that in the case of some desires it is events like thinking or judging which are central and not feelings.

In this chapter I shall give a brief account of desires and wants, placing particular emphasis on cases where the agent deliberates about his wants, either about what they are or about whether and how far to satisfy them. A difficulty for any account is the variety of ways in which words such as 'want' and 'desire' are used. It is not possible to draw a firm distinction between desires and wants: in some contexts it is appropriate to talk of the one, in some of the other. I can find little pattern in these different contexts, and I shall not make a distinction between them, but will use whichever word the context conventionally requires and mean no more by using the one term than the other. I shall be concerned only with those kinds of wants which are the grounds of action and which play a part in the explanations of actions. Even among these there is considerable variety. On the one hand there are very specific wants related to what one is immediately going to do: I want my steak rare, so that is the way I will cook it. On the other hand there are very general wants which do not seem related to particular actions: I want there to be greater equality between men and women. Again there are dispositional wants: my brother is always determined to get his own way. Compulsive wants, like an alcoholic's having such a craving for a drink that it compels him to break into an off-licence, may be contrasted with wants arrived at after evaluation and judgment, as when a school-leaver—after giving considerable thought to the matter—decides that he wants to take an engineering course.

To try and sort out all the vagaries of ordinary language would be profitless. Rather I shall try to give an account of a particular, though centrally important, kind of want. For reasons which will, I hope, become obvious, I shall call these feature-wants and characterise them by stating necessary and sufficient conditions for them. It might be said that feature-wants embody the minimum conditions that wants must have in order to explain. The Humean view would argue that the wants which are the grounds of action not only fulfil the conditions for feature-wants, but also certain further conditions. The controversial questions about wants are related to what these latter conditions are and whether all wants have to fulfil them. I shall argue in the next chapter that though some wants may fulfil some or all of them not all wants need to, and many of the wants which are the grounds of actions do not.

II—*The notion of a feature-want*

Let me explain why I use the term 'feature-want'. Suppose I act intentionally. In the absence of any accidental interventions I mean to do that which I am doing and it is this action rather than other possible actions which is intended. If that is so, then there are two possibilities. Firstly, it does not matter to me that I do this action rather than another. I have chosen arbitrarily: I have no reason for doing this action. This is not simply or even necessarily to say that I have no purpose which this action will help achieve, but that there is nothing about this action, no characteristic of the action, which makes me intend this action rather than any other. Such an action may be possible, though I find it strange, and it would not be typical of actions in general. It need not detain us here.

The second possibility is that it does matter to me that I do this action rather than another. It must have some feature or characteristic, absent in the other actions, which leads me to choose it. This feature may have been used to describe the action being performed, while other features irrelevant to its performance are not mentioned in its specification. Equally, it may not be part of the description but may only be mentioned in an explanation of the action. The fact that the action has this feature may constitute the agent's reason, or the presence of this feature in the action may cause the agent to do it. In all cases in which the agent performs an action because he thinks that it has this feature on its own or together with other relevant features, the agent wants to do an action which has the feature, and will be said to have a feature-want directed towards this feature of the action.

Consider an example: Jane Smith crosses the road. She may do so in order to avoid Mrs. Brown, or to buy a newspaper, or to get home as quickly as possible, or for a combination of these reasons. In each case a feature of the action of crossing the road is mentioned, and the explanation alleges that she crossed the road because crossing the road had that feature, because she wanted to do an action with that feature.

Features may be widely different in kind: they may relate to internal characteristics of the action, characteristics which the action itself has and can be seen to have; they may relate to characteristics it has in virtue of the agent's attitude towards it, as for instance if the agent wants to do an action because he believes it to be his duty; or they may be concerned with the consequences of the action. They may refer to states of mind, to states of affairs in the physical world, or to ways of acting. There is no limit to what may count as a feature, except that if it is to enter into a feature-want which gives rise to an action then the feature must be a characteristic of the action taken account of when the agent chooses it.

To spell out a want fully is often long-winded and unnatural; what is wanted is obvious enough without the feature wanted being given in full. Nevertheless it can be so given and it is necessary to do so to specify the general form of a feature-want. 'Patricia wants a new car' can be stated more fully as 'Patricia wants to bring about a state of affairs in which she has a motor-car'. 'Isabel wants a cigarette' is shorthand for 'Isabel wants a state of affairs to obtain in which she is smoking a cigarette'. 'Henry wants a state of affairs to obtain in which he feels he is loved' would more naturally be expressed by 'Henry wants love'. I shall therefore take a general statement of a feature-want, when spelt out fully to be of the form: 'X wants a state of affairs to obtain which has the feature P'.

It may look as if feature-wants are related only to rather specific features of possible actions the agent is considering in a given situation, while many of our wants are far more general and do not indicate any particular action for their satisfaction. Thus 'I want more money' may express a genuine want, even when I have no idea of any actions which would satisfy the want. However, it can still be expressed as a feature-want: I want to bring about a state of affairs which will enable me to acquire more money. This will define that feature of possible actions towards which I have a feature-want. How far such a general feature-want actually affects my action will depend on how important it is to me and on the presence or absence of competing feature-wants.

Equally the idea of a feature-want may not seem to take account of dispositional wants. But when an agent has such a want then what he has a disposition to have is, in fact, a feature-want, and in so far as dispositional wants seem to explain actions they do so because when the situation is appropriate the agent has the related feature-want. Thus I claim that dispositional wants can be dealt with in terms of feature-wants.

III—*Feature-wants relate to the future, have objects and involve pro-attitudes*

I shall now provide a definition of a feature-want by constructing a set of conditions which all feature-wants must fulfil. The first condition for a feature-want is that it must have an object. There must be something that is wanted— some feature that an action might have or might bring about. In some cases it may be that the agent does not know or is mistaken about what he wants and yet his wants still have objects. He may be dissatisfied and unsure about what would remove the dissatisfaction: he is sure he wants whatever will remove his dissatisfaction, even though he does not know what that is. In other cases the agent thinks he wants something, but finds it unsatisfying when he gets it: whatever he wanted, it was not what he thought he wanted. Or again, someone may think that he wants one feature of a possible state of affairs, while it is really quite another feature of the same state of affairs that he wants. For instance, I believe I want to help a friend for his sake while in reality I want the self-gratification which would result from giving the help. Nevertheless in all such cases there is something wanted: the want has an object.

The second condition relates to the object of the want. The characterisation of a feature-want given in the previous section requires the object to be that a certain state of affairs obtains. Often it may seem as if wanting is linked with lacking or being without something, so that the object must be that a state of affairs obtains which has a feature which does not characterise the present state of affairs. To say that I want a car seems to imply that I have not got one and want to bring about a state of affairs in which I have one. But there are examples where we appear to want what we have got or want to do what we are doing, such as a wealthy man wanting money. Although it is possible to make bringing about a change in what obtains a condition for a feature-want, it seems to me preferable to say that the feature mentioned in the object only needs to characterise a future state of affairs whether or not it characterises the present. There are apparent exceptions. Roger might say, when he is in London, that he wants to be in China. I shall rule out such exceptions by stipulation. The last example is not of a feature-want, but should, perhaps, be classified as a wish. It is therefore a condition for a feature-want that its object should be the obtaining of a future state of affairs with a specific feature.

It may be objected that this is rather a static model for wanting and that it fails to cover wanting to do things as well as wanting to have them. However, if 'state of affairs' is taken in a wide sense, both wanting to drive a new car as well as wanting to have it are covered. My wanting to drive the new car is rephrased as my wanting the state of affairs to obtain in which I am driving it.

The third condition is that an agent must have some kind of favourable attitude to what is wanted obtaining or unfavourable attitude to what is wanted not obtaining. A variety of different attitudes is possible, but each must be a favourable attitude, or what has been called a pro-attitude.[2] If some feature of an action is to be the ground of an agent doing it, then he must not be against that feature, or not more against its presence than its absence.

Consider first an example of a voluntary action: Helen is looking in a shop window; then there must be some aspect of so looking at this time which has led her to do it: there must be some reason for her choosing to do this rather than anything else. She may be doing it because she is waiting for a friend, because she sees some china she is thinking of buying, because she is watching the reflection of someone on the other side of the road. Any or all of these can constitute an explanation because each mentions some aspect or condition of her action which has led her to do it. In each case she forms a preference for her action because it has the feature wanted. In some cases she may have considered and rejected alternatives which lacked the feature. In other cases no such comparison may have been made. Of course there is not just one action which has the desirable feature. It follows that her feature-want is directed towards a class of actions all members of which share the feature towards which she has a pro-attitude. That pro-attitude is an essential part of the feature-want. She looks in the window because she is in favour of waiting for a friend, of looking at the china, or of watching the person on the other side of the road.

There is one possible explanation of her looking in the window which may seem to fit uneasily with the account being given. It is that she is looking just because she wants to and there is no special feature of looking which leads her to look. However, even here there is a feature of the action which is wanted, and that is the feature already mentioned in saying what the action is, the feature of looking in the window. In order to specify the action being explained, we usually have to refer to one of its features, and if it is that very feature towards which the want that explains the action is directed, then an answer of the type 'because she wants to' is the only possible response to a demand for an explanation. Why does she do this action, this action being identified as the one with the feature of looking in the window? The explanation is that the action has the feature mentioned, that feature is favoured and it was not in virtue of any other feature of the action that the agent did it.

What has been said so far about this condition has related to actions for which the agent has a feature-want which she chooses to satisfy or in which she has chosen freely. But what about actions, such as the actions of an alcoholic or a kleptomaniac, which the agent did not choose and could not help doing? Unless such actions are intentional they cannot be explained or motivated by wants or desires. When they are intentional but not voluntary there must have been some feature of the action which led the agent to do it: his want or desire for that feature must have caused or compelled him to do it. In such cases he must equally have a pro-attitude, even if it is of a different kind from that found in voluntary actions.

It may be argued that a feature-want as so far characterised would not, when used in giving an explanation, provide a sufficient condition for the agent to have acted in the way he did and in no other way. It may be true that if he had not had such a feature-want he would not have acted in the same way. Nevertheless even with that feature-want he might have acted in a different way: the action may be one way of achieving something the agent wants, but it is not the only way. A feature-want is directed towards a class of actions all of which have the feature in common. There is no reason why this class should have only one member. Thus in most cases the feature-want, which is the ground for the agent doing or deciding on a specific action, could be satisfied in other ways. If Jane wants to get a paper and as a result crosses the road, then, though the want may explain her crossing the road, it does not explain why she crossed the road at that particular place and at that particular time. But if the feature-want is to determine this action and this action alone and thus provide the explanation of why she did what she did and not anything else, it must exclude all other possible actions. Her wanting to get a paper does not explain why she did this action of crossing the road and no other. It merely explains why she did one of the actions which belong to the class of those enabling her to get a paper. Thus, it is claimed, a feature-want can only give a partial explanation.

Much of this argument is correct, but I do not think it damages the idea of a feature-want. Let us see why not. When a particular feature-want is given in explanation of an action, the range of actions which it would explain is limited by the existence of other feature-wants, even though these may be unstated. Some of the class of actions which would satisfy the feature-want would be ruled out by the fact that these actions have other features towards the avoidance of which the agent has a feature-want. There may be many different ways of getting to a friend's house, but some of them might involve danger or too much physical effort. In giving an explanation of an action it is unnecessary to state many of the feature-wants which would have excluded other actions which have the feature in question. However, there is no reason to suppose that these other feature-wants limit the class of actions in question to one action. We are likely to be left with a number of actions all of which would have equally satisfied the relevant feature-wants.

Is it ever possible, then, to have the required sufficient conditions for the action? Can we ever explain why this and only this particular action has been done? Can the agent's feature-wants ever completely determine his action? Is it not the case that all we can ever explain is why one of the actions having the feature mentioned and lacking the undesirable features has been performed? The answers to these questions depend on what is to count as a distinct action. We characterise an action by mentioning some of its features and in practice not many would be mentioned. Rarely—if ever—will an action be uniquely individuated by its description when considered independently of the context of the action. In the case of Jane Smith crossing the road slight differences of time and space will be immaterial and would not be noticed by her unless they introduced new features to the action. Actions which only varied so slightly would not be thought of as different actions and an agent would not want any one of them more than the others. All he wants to do is an action which has certain features, and within the range of actions fulfilling such conditions it is immaterial which he chooses; in fact to most agents all such actions will almost always be viewed as the same action. Thus it is unimportant that we do not have sufficient conditions for the particular action. When acting, the various actions which would satisfy a feature-want are not necessarily noticed as different. The agent merely does any action which will satisfy it so long as the action has no undesirable features.

IV—*Feature-wants as action-guiding*

Three conditions for feature-wants have been mentioned so far. The first related to the want having an object; the second stated that the object of the want is the obtaining or occurring of a state of affairs with a specific feature; the third was that the agent must have some kind of pro-attitude towards the feature. These conditions seem merely to indicate that the agent must like or approve of something he has not got or of some possible state of affairs. In some cases it seems as if wanting is no more than that, perhaps because typical of these cases are ones in which what is said to be wanted is unobtainable and so it makes no difference to the agent's actions whether he wants or merely likes. But wanting is more than liking. To want something is not just to judge the object of the want, or to have an attitude towards it. There is clearly some element of action-guiding, of a pull towards or attraction to what is wanted. 'The primitive sign of wanting is *trying to get*'.[3] Thus a fourth condition must be added: if an agent has a feature-want then he will try—subject to certain provisos— to bring about any state of affairs which has the feature to which the feature-want is directed. He will try to do what will satisfy the want so long as it is possible to satisfy it and unless he has reasons against doing so. Thus if someone claimed to have a feature-want and made no effort to bring about any state of affairs which had that feature, then some explanation would be expected. If no explanation in terms of competing feature-wants were forthcoming then there would be justification for denying that the agent did in fact have that feature-want. The normal case in which an agent does not try to get what he claims to want is where any achievable state of affairs which would have the feature wanted also has other features which are not wanted. If the resolution of all the relevant feature-wants points to a certain action and the agent does not do it, then either he is unable to do it or there must be a want which has not been taken account of.

But this condition is not sufficient. There are situations in which all the four conditions I have given are met and yet the agent does not want the feature mentioned. He may appear to be acting so that the feature may obtain; but even though he is in favour of the feature it may be incidental to getting what he wants. Joseph Appleby has a next-door neighbour, Mrs. Grump, whom he dislikes and whom he enjoys upsetting. He is going to play his trumpet, which he knows Mrs. Grump dislikes. Then, on this evidence, the four conditions seem to be fulfilled for him to be wanting to upset her: he is not at present upsetting her and will upset her when he plays. He enjoys upsetting her, and he is trying to do an action which has the feature of upsetting her. However in these circumstances he may claim that, though he is not sorry to be upsetting Mrs. Grump, that was not what he wanted. What he wanted was simply to practise his trumpet. Whether or not he is right in his claim, it is a possibility and it can be argued that the conditions do not, in these circumstances, allow a distinction between wanting to upset his neighbour and merely being glad that his neighbour is being upset.

To make this distinction we need to add a fifth condition. For the agent to have a feature-want not only must he favour a state of affairs in which the feature obtains but also the fact that he believes the feature will obtain must be sufficient for him, in the absence of competing feature-wants, to try to bring about that state of affairs.

These last two conditions may also be expressed in terms of the connection between wants and motivation. To say that an agent has a feature-want directed towards an action with a certain feature is to say that the agent is *prima facie* motivated to do the action by its having that feature. The agent will have a feature-want directed towards a feature if, and only if, the presence of the feature in a possible state of affairs not only leads an agent to have a pro-attitude towards that state of affairs but also is sufficient to motivate him to bring about that state of affairs. To want something implies being motivated towards acting to get it. One may like something without being so motivated, and so one may like something one has not got without wanting it.

In the light of what I said at the beginning of this chapter there now arises the question of whether an agent is necessarily conscious of his feature-wants. I said nothing explicitly about this in the conditions and this is intentional. Of course there can be argument about what being conscious involves: Does the agent have to have formulated his feature-want in order to be conscious of it? This need not delay us. Whichever answer is given I allow the possibility of an agent having a feature-want without being conscious of it. Nevertheless I take the central cases to be those in which the agent knowingly has a feature-want. It may not be in the centre of his attention; but it is implicit in his thinking, and an introspective examination of his thinking would reveal it. In the non-central cases a feature-want may be attributed to an agent by himself or others on the grounds of his behaviour, because his behaviour is what it would have been if he knowingly had had a feature-want. Thus the notion of a feature-want could not get its sense without the central cases, but nevertheless it covers the cases in which awareness of having the feature-want is absent.

This completes my account of the idea of a feature-want. According to the Humean view, wants and desires must satisfy certain further conditions. I shall argue in the next chapter that in this the Humean view is wrong; that the notion of a feature-want is sufficient to provide for the motivational and the explanatory rôles of wants; that none of the further conditions mentioned by the Humean is necessarily linked with the five I have outlined; and that, while some wants satisfy these additional conditions, others do not.

IV
Are All Feature-wants Humean-desires?
I—*The conditions for Humean-desires*
An account of wants or desires can be derived from Hume's theory of the passions, according to which wants are internal states of the agent—states akin to feelings—which are caused and which in their turn are the direct causes of action. I shall call any want which this account fits a Humean-desire. Thus the Humean would claim that all feature-wants are Humean-desires. Though I would not deny that some may be, I shall argue that there is no necessity for any feature-want to have any of the additional characteristics of Humean-desires.

For Hume desires are one kind of passion, and he sees a close connection between passions and sensations. They are both a kind of impression, the difference between them being that sensations are primary or original impressions derived from unknown sources, while passions are secondary impressions which 'are such as proceed from some of these original ones, either immediately or by the interposition of its idea'.[1] They might be said to be distinguished simply by their having different kinds of causes. Hume's claim that passions are 'original facts and realities compleat in themselves'[2] might suggest an interpretation of the passions as immediate feelings, as almost internal sensations. However, when Hume identifies the passions with impressions he makes it clear that such impressions are not inner sensations: a passion is an impression of reflection rather than an impression of sensation (though this contrast is not entirely clear). Whatever else it may be, a passion is undoubtedly something we are directly aware of and it is neither rational nor considered.

It is possible to see the passions as no more than a kind of internal feeling, almost like forces we feel pushing us towards action. The suggestion that the passions are felt forces certainly corresponds to some of our introspections about our passions or desires, particularly those expressed by metaphors such as 'bursting with anger', 'driven by desire', or 'consumed by passion'. It is not uncommon to feel forced to do something against one's will by the strength of one's desire, or to feel that one can only overcome some desire by a great effort of will. There are other cases in which desires seem to involve an internal sensation. For instance, as I mentioned earlier (Chapter III, Section III), someone can claim to have a desire and yet not know what the object of the desire is. She has a feeling which she dislikes and which she believes would disappear if the unknown object of the desire were obtained. Similarly someone can be mistaken about what it is he desires. He thinks it is one thing, only to discover when that is obtained that his desire is not satisfied. In these examples the desire seems to correspond to a certain feeling of excitement, discomfort, dissatisfaction or even pain. Thus at first sight it looks as if at least some desires are a kind of inner sensation, a feeling of emptiness which is at the same time a feeling of an inner force or drive which impels one towards action. Examples are hunger, thirst or sexual desire. In such cases it is perfectly proper to talk about the strength of the desire, the desire being more or less strong according to the force we feel exerted on us to satisfy the desire. Thus one condition for Humean-desires is that they involve the presence of a certain type of introspectible feeling, an awareness of being drawn to the object.

For Hume having a passion is an immediate and unconsidered reaction to a situation. There might appear to be exceptions, as when an agent realises that something is the means to the object of an already existing want and so wants that means. But the latter want need not be arrived at by thinking about the object of the want. The realisation of what is the means causes the agent to have the want, and the want is an immediate reaction to the new situation in which the agent now realises what is the means to the end. Thus a Humean-desire is a response to a stimulus, a response which occurs without the agent having any choice, or without his in any way contriving to respond in this way. The stimulus may be something one is aware of: seeing someone smoke immediately makes the smoker want to smoke. But equally the stimulus that produces the desire may be unknown: a pregnant woman has a craving for shrimps, but the craving is something which can spontaneously occur even without her having thought about shrimps. Thus Humean-desires have causes which in some cases are the idea of the object of the desire, but in other cases are more obscure and unknown. Even where they are unknown, there seems little reason to deny that they have causes. The second of these additional conditions for Humean-desires—that such desires have causes independent of the agent's volition—not only accords with the Humean view of desires but is also implicit in other accounts of desires. I shall call those feature-wants which satisfy this second condition impulse-desires; they may or may not satisfy the other conditions for Humean-desires.

Finally, there is the question of the connection between desires and the actions which satisfy them. For the Humean this is a causal link. Desires are causes of action: any action is produced as a result of the different desires acting on the agent. Though they may pull in different directions, the desires will resolve themselves so that the strongest desire will cause the action. Moreover the strength of a desire is intrinsic to the desire itself and does not result from the judgment or decision of the agent. The strongest desire is not the desire the agent thinks most important, for its strength is not under the agent's control. Thus the last of these additional conditions for Humean-desires is that desires directly cause actions and are the only possible internal psychological determinants of those actions.

II—*The case of Matthew Dyer*

In order to examine the question of whether all feature-wants must satisfy the additional conditions for Humean-desires let us look at an example. Suppose we are told that Matthew Dyer has a great desire to see the Taj Mahal, that he is scrimping and saving to get the money to get there and that much of what he does seems to relate to the satisfying of this desire. We are convinced that the conditions for a feature-want are satisfied. However, I suggest, from this information we cannot tell how the desire originated, how it feels to him or how it is related to his actions. His desire may have been formed as a result of much thought and deliberation: it may depend on what seems to be evaluation and reasoning. His desire to see the Taj Mahal may have been formed after reading or thinking about it, weighing up what he might get out of seeing it, and what he might have to sacrifice in order to see it. It seems to him that only after he has gone through certain processes of thought does he make up his mind that this is what he wants to do.

At the other extreme it is possible that no thought at all was involved. It may have been that on the first occasion on which he had any idea of the Taj Mahal he immediately felt an overwhelming desire to see it. It may simply have been the sound of its name, some description of it, or how a friend reacted to it which produced the desire. These were stimuli to which the desire was an immediate reaction.

So much for the different ways his desire might originate. Equally Matthew Dyer might describe his desire by reporting different introspections about it. On the one hand, he might simply say that he knows he wants to see the Taj Mahal, having arrived at this decision after deliberating; that he is aware that the desire is of a kind which satisfies the five conditions for feature-wants; that he has a cognition of his want, but that there is no feeling attached to it. On the other hand he might describe feelings of being driven, impelled, forced, or drawn towards the object of his desire.

Consider next the different ways in which his desire to see the Taj Mahal might relate to his future actions. It might be the case that the desire felt so strong that he was unable to do anything but try to satisfy it. In such a case it would be said that his desire was obsessive, compulsive or uncontrollable, and that once he had the desire the actions aimed at getting to see the Taj Mahal necessarily followed. Or it might seem that to a greater or lesser extent Matthew Dyer decided, either negatively—by not interfering with his natural reaction to having the desire—or positively—by making a definite decision that he should act so as to satisfy the desire.

It may be a desire which he balances against other desires or one which, though strong, can be controlled; whichever is the case he chooses whether or not to satisfy it.

The brief description of Matthew Dyer's desire with which I began is consistent with various possibilities in relation to its origination, to how it felt and to how it related to consequential actions. With further information we might be able to decide which of these possible accounts of his desire is correct. But, as they stand, only in some of these accounts does the desire fulfil the conditions for a Humean-desire. If the account of the desire suggests that he has deliberated in deciding on it, or that there was no introspectible feeling, or that he could control it, then it looks as if the conditions are not satisfied. The Humean has then either to abandon some of these conditions or to show that the failure to satisfy them is mere appearance and misleading as to the true nature of the desire. He has to show that all the possible kinds of desire which Matthew Dyer might have had are equally reducible to a more or less complex form of a desire in which the conditions are satisfied. I want now to look in more detail at the way exceptions to the conditions seem to arise and see whether the Humean is right.

III—*Do feature-wants involve an ontrospectible feeling?*

Of the conditions for Humean-desires which the Humean alleges must hold for all desires, consider first the condition that a Humean-desire involves some kind of introspectible feeling. As I have said before, this has been the source of some of the main challenges to the Humean view. But there are ways in which the Humean might defend himself and show that, though in a particular desire there might appear to be no such feeling, it is nevertheless present. Two sorts of counter-example to the condition need explanation. In the first the action—though intentional—is immediate, as when a driver responds to an emergency by braking hard. The agent will not have thought about what he wants and may not even be aware that he has a desire, though an observer would infer one. In such cases (to be discussed in Chapter XI)

I suggest that the agent has a feature-want whether or not he has either a Humean- or an impulse-desire.

My concern here is rather with a type of case in which the agent has no introspectible feeling and yet is aware of what he is doing and of what he wants in doing it. The most obvious case is where the agent may be said to form his own wants. One of the possible accounts of Matthew Dyer's desire is an example. Others vary from the trivial to the vitally important. One person deliberately avoids the motorway in driving from London to Birmingham and thus has a desire to drive by his chosen route rather than by any other. Someone else wants to train as a teacher. Another person wants to take out a comprehensive insurance on his house. Yet another wants to support a political system based on a mixed economy. All of these wants may be taken as leading to action. Some of them are of no great consequence and it might be argued that they are so trivial that the desires are not strong enough for any feeling to register. In the more significant cases the Humean might argue that a natural way to describe such wants would be to say that the agents feel strongly or even passionately about what they want. Only if a feeling were involved could wants be described in this way. In some cases there is a feeling, though it is not always a feeling of being impelled towards the object of the want. An agent may, for example, feel pleasure at the thought of the object of the want. It is a feeling which the agent might have even if he had no want.

In many cases there is not even this kind of feeling; there is nothing corresponding to a Humean impression. What is meant by 'feel' in 'feeling strongly' in the context of wants is close to that sense of 'feel' in which it is akin to thinking or believing—'I feel you ought to go to the meeting'. Here strength of feeling refers to the strength of conviction with which one holds the opinion. In the same way strength of feeling about a want can refer to what one thinks about the object of the want, to the fact that the want is to be given high priority or is to carry great weight in deliberating or to the extent to which one is, or thinks one ought to be, committed to trying to satisfy that want.

It is points such as these which partly concern Hume when he distinguishes between calm and violent passions. A calm passion is, as Ardal emphasises, 'a passion which *on most occasions* involves low emotional intensity'.[3] As Hume says: 'Now 'tis certain, there are certain calm desires and tendencies, which, tho' they be real passions, produce little emotion in the mind and are more known by their effects than by the immediate feeling or sensation'.[4] So it seems that it is the strength of feeling or emotion which makes the difference between calm and violent passions. But the strength of feeling is not a measure of the extent to which a passion is likely to influence action. Hume distinguishes between 'a calm and a weak passion; betwixt a violent and a strong one'.[5] He does not think that strength of emotion is either necessary to a passion or is what determines action. One interpretation is to see calmness or violence as being related to the pro-attitude, and weakness or strength of feeling as being related to the attempt to satisfy the desire.

In much of this Hume seems to me to be right, though it is difficult to relate what he says in this respect to his original characterisation of the passions. If he is going to argue that reason itself cannot determine action, but that the passions must, then he requires a rather different notion of the passions from the one he begins with. It is not sufficient to define the passions as impressions of reflection. For it is far from clear what impression is present in a calm passion. The fact that a passion may be more known by its effect than by the immediate feeling suggests that there need be no introspective way of recognising it. We have thus two contrasting notions of a passion. According to the first it is an impression, an original existent, something of which one is directly aware: it is that which is calm or violent. According to the second it is that which gives rise to actions, is known by its effects, is inferred from there being an intentional action, and is strong or weak. The first notion suggests an introspectible feeling as essential: the second suggests it is unnecessary. On the Humean view the first notion is an attempt to give an account of what passions having the function defined by the second must be. But need the two notions be connected? The remarks Hume makes about calm passions suggest they need not be.

But one must not jump to the conclusion that, if an introspectible feeling need not be present, then nothing which is introspectible need be present. In the case of many wants which lack any element of feeling it is quite clear that the agent is thinking, and that what he is doing in thinking constitutes part of his want. But I shall not try to argue that some kind of conscious event is essential to a want. Even if this could be shown the variety of possible events would be so great that it would not be particularly useful. What is important for my argument is that an introspectible feeling is not essential to a want.

IV—Feature-wants and causality

There remain two further conditions which the Humean alleges must be satisfied by all desires or wants: firstly a desire must have a cause independent of the agent's volition and secondly desires must be causes of actions. From the example of Matthew Dyer it is clear that, though some of the possible forms his desire might take would fulfil these conditions, other forms appear not to fulfil them. The Humean would argue that in such cases it is not the conditions which are at fault but rather it is the appearance of not fulfilling them which is misleading. It is not simply that in such cases the desire is in fact different from what it seems, but that it must be different, that a desire of the form suggested is an impossibility.

While allowing that on particular occasions appearances may be deceptive, I have found no satisfactory argument for their always being deceptive. There is nothing in the nature of feature-wants as so far outlined which implies that if the first group of conditions is satisfied then these additional conditions must also be satisfied, nor is there anything to suggest any contradiction in a feature-want failing to satisfy the latter conditions. The Humean view gains its plausibility from the apparent absence of any alternative to it in the way desires might originate, or in the way they might be related to actions. I shall develop such an alternative in chapter VI.

For the moment I only want to make one or two points about the way the Humean deals with what appear to be counter-examples to his view.

If Matthew Dyer's desire to see the Taj Mahal is both an immediate reaction to a stimulus and also forces him to act so as to satisfy the desire, then certainly the Humean account fits. But in other cases, as I suggested earlier, it looks as if these further conditions are not satisfied. The desire may have been arrived at after thought and deliberation. Matthew Dyer may have decided that what he wanted was to see the Taj Mahal, and thus the desire appears not to have originated independently of his volition. Further it may seem that he chose whether or not to satisfy his desire, even if the desire had a causal origin. Such a choice makes it look as if his desires were not the causes of his actions.

What account would the Humean give of the reality that lies behind this appearance? Consider first the question of origin, and the possibility that deliberation allows there to be a non-causal origin. A Humean does not deny that an agent can think about what to do, but claims that such reasoning as can take place is not incompatible with desires being caused. The generally accepted view of reasoning is that it must either be deductive or causal: reasoning can show a conceptual or empirical connection between the objects of desires and thus may give rise to a new desire. But in each case the formation of a desire depends on a previously given desire. The reasoning must start with some wants or desires of the agent as premisses. These latter cannot but originate causally, and with causes that are independent of the agent's volition. That those desires occur is just a fact about the agent. They are not the kind of thing which he can bring about or choose to have. When we seem to be deciding what we want we are either inferring new wants from old wants, or we are merely observing ourselves and discovering what it is we want. The kind of thing which can satisfy the conditions for feature-wants must arise, directly or indirectly, as something which happens to the agent.

It sometimes seems possible to control a desire or to choose whether or not to satisfy a desire. Here some

Humeans would allege that what is really happening is that there are conflicting desires. When one controls a desire it means that one has a competing desire which is stronger. How one acts must be determined by which of one's desires is the stronger, and conflicts between one's desires can only be resolved in the way conflicts between opposing forces are resolved. Some of those who take a causal view of the origination of actions would argue differently, claiming that desires can both be the causes of action and yet be under the control of the agent. I have more sympathy with this last approach in that it does not deny the possibility of exercising choice over one's desires. However the sense in which desires can be causes in this way is a special one and not without problems, problems I shall discuss in Chapter X.

V—*Assumptions behind the Humean view of feature-wants*
The way a Humean deals with those cases of wants and desires which appear to be incompatible with his account depends on four views with which I disagree. The first is that deliberation or thinking in relation to action is limited to deductive and causal reasoning. In Chapter VI I shall argue that there are other kinds of thinking and reasoning which are not merely contemplative, but are designed to come to a conclusion. Such alternative methods of reasoning may be used in the formation of wants and thus lead to a different view from the Humean about feature-wants.

The second view is that what an agent wants must be a fact about him in the same way as being allergic to cats is a fact about someone: the idea of choosing or deciding on what one is to want does not, it is alleged, make sense. There are, of course, some kinds of wants which do not originate through choice. I do not choose to be hungry; the pregnant woman does not choose to have a craving for shrimps. The smoker does not choose to want a cigarette. It cannot be denied that it sounds odd to suggest that someone decided to have a particular desire. Those wants that we most usually refer to as desires cannot be instigated by the agent who has them. But what is true of these impulse-desires need not be true of the whole range of wants. Would it not do an injustice to the facts to say that Matthew Dyer's want could not have been the result of deliberation or choice? It seems to me impossible to maintain both that wants are a required element in the motivation of action, and that they cannot be open to decision. It may be that as a matter of contingent fact all wants are Humean-desires in this respect. What I am arguing for is that it is not true *a priori*.

One part of this view which I am questioning is that all pro-attitudes must be reduced to a kind of feeling or impression. For instance in Hume's view evaluating is having a feeling of a certain sort. Such a view was no doubt the result of a reaction against rationalist theories of morality, but a non-objectivist view of morality does not need to reduce morality to feeling. To do so leaves out, among other things, the element of committing oneself in assenting to an evaluation. Such notions, I shall argue, are central not only to morality and moral evaluation but also to those feature-wants we can identify with reasons for action. The failure to allow any place for these elements in its notion of wants is one of the major limitations of the Humean account.

The third view which is implicit in a Humean way of dealing with these apparent counter-examples is not unrelated to seeing desires as essentially occurrences. It is that actions depend on the strongest desire, and that where an agent acts in a way that does not satisfy what appears to be his desire it must be because of the existence of a stronger desire. I have already discussed part of this view in considering whether wants or desires necessarily involve some feeling. I suggested that what we call strength of feeling does not relate to any internal impression, and that it is difficult to identify in all cases the relative strength of different desires unless we are allowed to infer their strength from the way the agent acts. It is possible to allow a notion of strength if the strength of a desire can depend on the agent's evaluation of that desire, and if a conflict between such desires can be seen not only as forces operating against each other, but also as related to rational processes of evaluation that the agent makes.

The fourth view is that wants lead inevitably to action

without there being any possibility of the agent's intervening in the process leading from his having a want to his acting on it. It may be suggested that if an agent has a feature-want, whether caused or chosen, he is already committed *prima facie* to trying to bring about a state of affairs with that feature. It might seem as if the agent's decision about whether or not to satisfy his feature-want is already made and thus that there is no room for the evaluation of his desires. This is not the case; that he has a feature-want commits him to an action only in the absence of conflicting feature-wants. Thus he has still got a decision to make about the weight to attach to the feature-want in relation to other feature-wants. Moreover, it is still possible for him to consider other aspects of the situation and form new feature-wants against which the original one has to be evaluated. A decision about how to act will not follow until he has evaluated all the feature-wants he is caused to have or has decided to have. That decision can always be revised, until it is no longer possible for him to form and take account of new feature-wants—that is until he has acted on that decision.

Let me briefly try to indicate what I am claiming. I have suggested that a notion of a feature-want can be developed such that all intentional action results from a feature-want which must fulfil certain minimal conditions, the most important being that there must be a pro-attitude towards a possible state of affairs, and that the pro-attitude is sufficient to motivate the agent to act so as to bring about that state of affairs. A feature-want does not imply any particular idea of how it originates. It may be a reaction to a stimulus or it may be the result of a decision by the agent. Further a feature-want suggests nothing about the relation of a feature-want to an action except that to have a feature-want implies that the agent would, all things being equal, try to satisfy the want. Feature-wants may or may not cause the action directly.

The account I have given allows a three-fold division of feature-wants. Firstly, there are feature-wants which may be said to be both caused and to be the causes of action. They are caused in that they are a response to a stimulus arising unbidden and not as a result of thought and evaluation. They are causes in the sense that they compel the agent to act in order to satisfy them, and leave him no choice about whether to do so. These are what I call compulsive desires. Secondly, there are feature-wants which are caused in the same way as are those of the first type, but which have a different relation to the actions which satisfy them. Rather than compelling action, they are subject to the control of the agent. He cannot choose whether or not to have them: they are like forces pushing him in the direction of the action, but are forces he can choose whether or not to resist. Typical of these feature-wants is thirst and I have called them impulse-desires. Thirdly, there are feature-wants which are not caused, but are formed by the agent, chosen by him and often the result of evaluation and deliberation: further, they are satisfied as the result of the choice of the agent. He does not feel pushed in the direction of the action, rather he decides to push himself.

The Humean would clearly deny that feature-wants of the last type are possible. Moreover he would seem to suppose that all impulse-desires—though to be distinguished from compulsive desires—are equally the causes of action, and not subject to evaluation by the agent. This leads to a difficulty in distinguishing between different types of causes. Hume seems to use a distinction between external and internal causes which I do not find satisfactory. I would claim that my account enables a more satisfactory distinction to be made and serves as the basis for an adequate understanding of the ways actions originate. But much that is required to justify this claim still remains to be argued.

V
Practical Reasoning

I—*The problem*

In this chapter and the next I want to consider the actual process of deliberating. This may be described as one of moving from premises to a conclusion, though I prefer to describe it in terms of moving from a problem to its solution. In deliberating about what to do—in these chapters I shall limit myself to practical deliberation—an agent sets himself to find an answer to his problem, thus deciding what to do. The full statement of the problem will involve giving all the relevant information, and—according to the Humean —this gives us the premises from which we can deduce a conclusion which is the solution. All reasoning, the Humean claims, must either be deductive or inductive—the results of induction giving us, when added to what we directly observe, the required information for the statement of the practical problem.

In characterising the Humean view in this way I contrast induction with deduction[1] not by saying that an inductive argument is a non-deductive one, but rather by taking an inductive argument to be one which establishes a factual generalisation on the basis of particular instances, and thus provides us with the causal knowledge required to make any estimation of the means required to achieve a particular end. By 'deduction' I mean demonstrative reasoning, reasoning in which the conclusion is entailed by the premises: if the premises are true then necessarily the conclusion is also true. What is given in the premises is sufficient to give a complete and, if the premises are accepted, an unchallengeable justification of the conclusion. I do not limit a deductive argument to one which is logically justified, because of doubts about the characterisation of logic. Nor do I want to exclude certain types of argument such as Hare's imperative inference[2] or those which Kenny thinks conform to a logic of satisfactoriness.³

In this chapter my purpose is to criticise the Humean view that in practical deliberation the only form of reasoning is deduction, except in so far as induction may be required to establish causal knowledge. In doing so my aim is not to criticise any view actually held, but is to point to the limitations of deduction and to provide something with which to contrast my own view of deliberation.

II—*The different contrasts for decision-making*

The Humean view seems to assume that the normal, if not the only, decision-making context is one in which all that is needed is a decision about how to achieve a given end or purpose. All the agent has to do is to select the appropriate causal information, apply it to his present situation, and thus deduce a conclusion about what to do. Suppose I want to drive from London to Cambridge and have to decide which route to take. Here it is not wholly implausible to construct a piece of reasoning such as the following:

> I want to get from London to Cambridge
> The A10 is the best road from London to Cambridge
> So I should take the A10.

This could be expanded so as to state the characteristics of the A10 which makes it the best route and to show the desirability of these characteristics to me. But it would remain in the same form.

Arguments of this and similar types have been studied in great detail.⁴ Whether the conclusion of such arguments should be taken as an action, an imperative or a statement is a matter for argument, as is the nature of the logical relation between the premisses and the conclusion. I shall not pursue these matters here. However, such patterns of inference only apply to a relatively restricted number of contexts, contexts in which there is a clearly established purpose, and only one means of achieving it. Where there is more than one means, and the agent is called on to choose between them, such a pattern does not provide an adequate account.

On many occasions an agent has to choose between alternatives without having a definite end in mind. It is not a matter of finding the best means to a given end: rather in so far as ends are appropriate to the decision it is a matter of finding which ends are relevant to each of the alternatives and how far each is accomplished. Suppose someone is faced with choosing among candidates in an election, whether the election is parliamentary or for membership of the committee of a small voluntary organisation. He might in such a situation be fairly sure about what he wants the government or the committee to achieve, and thus all he has to decide is which of the candidates seems most likely to help the achievement of that end. On the other hand he might not be so sure, and yet feel he has an obligation to vote. Before he deliberates he might be uncertain about what the government or committee should be trying to do, and part of his deliberation would involve deciding about just that. Indeed it can be argued that no reasonable decision about voting could be made until that question was settled.

Take another example: before setting out for a drive, we may have no definite plan. We first have to decide where we want to go, and in making that decision we may not have any definite purpose, such as finding some rare plant. All we know is that we want an enjoyable outing and that many different ones would be enjoyable. It is unclear what account the Humean would give of such deliberation, but it is difficult to see how it could consist of deduction.

We have thus a variety of decision-making contexts. We have at one extreme cases in which it is a matter of settling the means to a given end: at the other extreme we have to settle what our ends are to be. But in many cases we are faced with a situation in which action is demanded and questions of means and ends are so intertwined that they almost certainly cannot be unravelled. I shall argue that the Humean model not only cannot cope with those cases where ends have to be settled first, but cannot even cope with many of those cases which are a matter of finding the best means to an end the agent already has in mind.

Let us consider, then, examples of both extremes. Take first the case of Adrian Flower, who wants to prevent the building of a new road which would spoil a well-known beauty-spot and also disturb the peace of his country retreat. He has to work out the means by which he can accomplish a definite end. He has to discover the various legal processes he can use to get an inquiry instigated; he has to consider how to get support from other interested people and how to get publicity; he has to decide which kinds of arguments would appeal both to the media and to those in positions of influence. In such a case he begins with a very definite and precise purpose in mind, and it looks as if he has only to establish the relevant facts, estimate the likelihood of different outcomes, make judgments about the reactions of others, and then, using all this material, decide on what would be the most effective way of achieving his end. He may work out several different lines of approach, try to estimate the consequences of each, and thus calculate the probability of each leading to the road not being built. In such cases the probability does not need to be measurable. He merely has to be able to decide which line of approach is most likely to achieve his purpose, and that will be the one to be followed. Hence, in such a case of deliberation, it seems to be a matter of Adrian Flower having an end he wants accomplished, using causal reasoning to establish the means to that end, and deducing that he should do those actions specified as the means. His reasoning could even be formulated as a practical syllogism of a kind:

> I want to stop the road being built
> Actions A_1, A_2, . . . are the most likely way of stopping the road being built
> Therefore I should do actions A_1, A_2, . . .

This syllogism is not necessarily how Adrian Flower actually argues, but can be said to represent the structure of his argument.

Such an example of decision-making seems to be adequately accounted for by the Humean model of deliberation. It does not depend on the agent having any particular expertise. But cases which do, like an engineer working out how to bridge a river, an architect designing a factory, or a doctor deciding on the treatment of a patient, seem to be even better illustrations of the Humean view. In each case the agent is deliberating about what to do, and in so doing is merely calculating how to achieve, in the most efficient way, an end which he has already set himself. Thus the deliberation is reduced to factual deliberation.

Even in those cases which seem to provide the best illustrations of the Humean account, the situation is often not as simple as it appears. At every stage of the reasoning other factors than the tendency to achieve the one given end may be relevant. Indeed it is an exceptional case in which only one end is relevant. The agent may not recognise this: he may fail to pay attention to such other factors and could be criticised for this failure. On the other hand he may take account of them explicitly. Determining the extent to which he should let them affect the way he tries to achieve his given end is part of what may take place when he is reasoning. Clearly there are some things which very few would do even if their ends would be furthered, or even if the end could be best or only accomplished in this way. Consider again the case of Adrian Flower. However great his enthusiasm for his cause, it is unlikely he would consider, say, blowing up government offices, or even bother working out whether such an action would be effective. But there are less far-fetched means which he might consider, such as minor bribery, twisting the truth or the disruption of the inquiry into the project. In deciding whether or not to use such means it may not only be their effectiveness in getting the road abandoned on which his decision is based. He has to take account of the extent to which such means are wrong and also the undesirability of other consequences such as having to pay out money or making enemies. These factors have to be weighed against the value he attaches to getting the construction of the road stopped.

Equally the bridge-builder could—and certainly should—take into account many factors which are relevant to his decision about the bridge, and go beyond the question of what would be the most efficient bridge. He may be concerned with its beauty, with damage to the surrounding countryside, with different effects on traffic patterns which various designs might have or with the work-conditions of those building the bridge. Whether or not he actually takes these into account, it can be argued that they are relevant and that his deliberation is defective if they are not considered. Thus, though for some people on some occasions deciding which bridge to build might just involve causal and deductive reasoning, it would appear that for others it would be much more complex, and they would have to bring into relation with each other a variety of ends, wants or values.

No doubt a Humean would deal with these points by suggesting that, though they make the structure of the argument more complicated by adding further premises and additional steps in the deduction, they do not lead to any difference in kind between the reasoning needed in these cases and that needed in simpler cases. To examine such claims let us first look at what is assumed if it is suggested that the additional ends or wants merely have to be stated as part of the premises of the agent's deliberation. This seems to suggest that all the wants can be known or fixed in advance, that they are given as facts about the agent and are independent of the particular situation the agent is in. But this runs counter to the nature of wants.

In many cases an agent's wants, whether relatively definite or at the other extreme very unspecific, do not determine unambiguously what will satisfy them. Such wants are under-determined in a way that is analogous to the open-texture of meanings. What the agent will want in the situation must be determined as the situation arises and not before. Suppose a keen gardener wants to have a house with a large garden, and makes strenuous efforts to satisfy his want. It would be an unusual and unwise man who has a precise notion of the garden he wants and will only be satisfied by one which conforms to it. Most people in this circumstance would know they wanted a large garden, but would not be sure about the details. However specific anyone tries to be he is unlikely to be able to formulate his conditions in such a way that he can tell automatically whether a particular garden will satisfy his want, and thus a further decision about the nature of his want will be required. Unless he were wholly inflexible no statement of his prior wants will determine whether a particular garden will satisfy him. His wants become determined as they are faced with particular situations. They interact with what happens to him and the situations he finds himself in. An agent will either have to respond to the stimulus of a situation, or he will have to make a decision about what his wants are in this situation. This is not simply a matter of taking account of conflicting wants, it is a matter of discovering or deciding what it is that he wants.

This argument may be criticised on the grounds that it only relates to an account of the way people actually reason and not to the logical structure of the reasoning. Though it may be the case that no agent could state all his premisses before making any of his calculations, nevertheless, it is argued, if we are trying to reveal the logical structure of his deliberation we can state his premisses at the point in the deduction when they are needed, whether or not this corresponds to the point in his deliberation at which they were formulated.

But consider what this involves if one small complication is added to Adrian Flower's deliberation. Let us suppose that he has found that the only way to stop the road being built is by persuading a friend of his, J.K., who is a civil servant, to fake some of the figures about traffic flow in the area. He then has an inference in which the second premiss is: Persuading J.K. to alter the traffic flow figures will stop the road being built. The conclusion would suggest that he tries to persuade him. However, his deliberation is unlikely to be limited to this. He would have to ask himself about the acceptability of what he was asking J.K. to do, how wrong was his action in so asking and the effect of it on his friendship with J.K. He would then have to ask himself whether these factors would be balanced by the advantages of the road not being built. He would have to choose between the satisfaction of different wants and decide on a preference. Suppose he prefers the road not being built. Then it will be argued that this preference will be built into the argument, and a more complex form of the original argument will be obtained. But this is to suggest that the formation of the preference was not itself a matter for deliberation or reasoning. This suggestion must, it seems to me, be rejected, and later argument will suggest grounds for the claim that choice and the formation of preferences like the formation of wants can be a rational matter, and this very rationality is something the Humean view cannot account for.

At this point it might be argued that the Humean can appeal to decision theory to provide a model for the reasoning process. But decision theory has little or nothing to say about the formation of preferences. It is only applicable where the consequences of different possible actions can be accurately predicted, or at least the probability of their occurring can be estimated, and where the preferences of the agent for these consequences can be ordered. In some cases we do not have the required predictability or cannot measure the likelihood of alternative outcomes. In other cases to give an agent's preferences for alternative outcomes is an unsatisfactory way of showing how his wants relate to each other; most important of all, the decision theory model can give no account of the formation of preferences and the way they are ordered, and their formation is often an essential part of the agent's deliberation.

Thus my argument about these seemingly simple means-ends cases is that they are often not as simple as they seem, and involve factors which are not originally apparent. They involve choices, ordering of preferences, coming to a decision about what one wants in a particular situation. This is the type of context in which the Humean view seemed most plausible. What then about contexts at the other extreme?

Ann Elworthy is coming to the end of her school career,

and has to decide whether or not to try to go to the university. She might have some vague aim like wanting to live a happy and worthwhile life, but this would give little guidance. She needs to decide much more specifically about the kinds of things she wants to do in the long-term. Of course some of her interests or wants, some of the things she enjoys or thinks valuable, will be fixed prior to thinking about the decision. But the application of these to the particular problem will require thought and decision. Let us suppose she has already formed certain ambitions to gain power and money, but has also a concern for the welfare of the less well-off. She enjoys travelling and singing, and dislikes accepting routine or authority. In actual practice the picture might be even more complicated, and far more factors would be relevant. She has to choose between two possible actions, and she cannot settle it by asking which will better achieve a previously given aim. Unlike the previous type of case, choosing involves deciding just which of her interests are relevant, and even deciding what some of her interests are to be. Thus the deductive reasoning of the means-end case is not applicable in any straightforward way.

What then is the structure of the deliberation in cases such as that of Ann Elworthy? A Humean might try to distinguish four stages. In the first the agent ascertains what actions are available to her: in this case they are to try or not to try to go to the university. In the second stage an attempt would be made to discover the likely outcomes of each action: here she would try to see what possibilities would be opened up by going or not going to the university. The third stage would involve relating her wants to each action and its outcome, and then seeing how far they were satisfied. The fourth stage would be to arrive at that action which would maximise the satisfaction of her wants and interests.

Though it is difficult to see what account the Humean could give of the thinking involved in the first stage, I do not want to discuss it. Nor do I want to say more about the second stage than I have already said in Chapter II. It is what happens in the third and fourth stages which is important for my argument. I want to consider four sets of difficulties which result from separating these last two stages and from supposing that the thinking involved in them must be deductive—the first of these in the next two sections; the second and third in section IV; and the fourth in Section V.

III—*The practice of deliberating and suppressed premisses*

The first of these difficulties is one that has already cropped up several times and is fundamentally about the relation between any view or theory about deliberation and the way people actually deliberate. Anyone who advocated the Humean view would not consider it any disproof of their view that in thinking about what he was going to do an agent would rarely, if ever, go through the steps of a deductive argument. The Humean view is not attempting to describe how people actually arrive at decisions. Nor is the account of deliberation I am advocating trying to do this. Yet such accounts of deliberation must bear some relation to the way people actually deliberate.

Three models of the relation between the so-called logical structure of a piece of reasoning and the actual reasoning may repay examination. First, there is a model suggested by the idea of a suppressed premiss. Secondly, there is a model based on the idea that the logical structure is the structure which justifies the conclusion reached in the reasoning. Thirdly, there is a model related to the claim that the logical structure shows what anyone who reaches a particular conclusion must thereby be committing himself to.

Consider the first model. There is no doubt that in arguments we do not always state all the required steps. I may suppress a premiss, there being no need to state the obvious, though I am fully aware of it. Again I may, as in some arithmetical calculations, simply not notice a step taken because it is so obvious. In such cases the logical structure of a piece of reasoning is given by the reasoning being spelt out in full, by saying how the agent would have reasoned if he had taken more time, or if he had not thought some points so obvious that they did not need to be made explicit. In such cases the agent only reaches his conclusion because that conclusion follows logically from premisses, and the way the conclusion follows gives the logical structure. If the conclusion did not follow, and this were pointed out to the agent, then he would agree he had made a mistake in his thinking and would reject his conclusion in favour of a different one. Thus even if the logical reasoning did not occur explicitly, nevertheless the agent saw, or thought he saw, that the conclusion logically followed without it being necessary to go through all the steps formally needed to show how it followed. Such an agent if asked about his conclusion, either from the point of view of explanation or justification, would give the full argument embodying its logical structure rather than the shortened argument which his thinking actually followed.

However, the way an argument is completed by supplying a suppressed premiss is not uncontroversial. Such arguments, though they can be completed by supplying a premiss which makes the argument invalid, can also be completed by supplying one that makes the argument valid. For instance, if it is said that this piece of metal can be magnetised because it is iron, we naturally supply the additional premiss that all iron can be magnetised, rather than the premiss that some iron can be magnetised. We choose the former because the argument suggests that the conclusion follows, and that premiss makes the argument valid. In this example the supplying of the premiss in question rather than another is unexceptionable, and indeed any other choice would be wrong. In cases where the argument can be made valid by supplying a premiss which the arguer believes to be true, then that premiss must be supplied.

In other cases the choice of premiss to be added is not so obvious, especially in cases where we can either make the argument valid by supplying a false premiss or invalid by supplying a true premiss. Take the following example:

Medicine is a good career for John because it is well-paid.

To make this a valid argument we have to supply a premiss such as:

All careers which are well-paid are good careers for John.

Not everybody would accept the first argument, but even fewer would accept this additional premiss. On the other hand it will be invalid if a true premiss such as the following is supplied:

> Some careers which are well-paid are good careers for John.

How do we choose between these alternative ways of supplying a premiss? Which of them enables us to show the logical structure of the argument? In fact what is intended by someone who uses the original argument is probably different from both. A premiss such as the following may be closer to what is intended:

> Careers which are well-paid are likely to be good careers for John.

But the most this could justify would be the conclusion that medicine is likely to be a good career for John, and that is not the conclusion stated. We are no further forward in finding a suppressed premiss for the original argument. No premiss, I suggest, which tries to turn such an argument into deductive form will reveal the real structure of the argument. That structure is represented by following up the claim that the premiss is a good, though not conclusive or deductive, reason for the conclusion. Trying to show the structure of an argument by insisting that it must be deductive will, in many cases, simply change it into a different argument. Thus the model of a suppressed premiss does not support the Humean view.

IV—*Does deduction provide the standard for a good argument?*

According to the second model what is meant by saying that the real structure of deliberation is deduction is that it is by deduction that one ought to deliberate, that deduction provides a norm for deliberation, or that deduction provides the only method of arriving at justifiable conclusions or of justifying conclusions. In considering deliberation one is not interested in how people actually deliberate, because they make mistakes or in other ways deliberate inadequately. What one is interested in is how to deliberate correctly, how to reach conclusions that are justified by one's reasoning. A philosophical theory of deliberation cannot be empirical: it must be concerned with the idea of deliberation, with the principles of deliberation people should be trying to follow. Logic is essentially normative in that it gives the correct way of reasoning. What is true or false in logic is not dependent on how people argue, rather logic formulates the principles of how to argue correctly. Thus the claim about deliberation is that if you want to deliberate correctly, if you do not want the method of your deliberation to involve any mistakes, if you do not want the conclusions of your deliberation to be open to criticism on the grounds of the way you deliberated, then you must use deductive reasoning.

This view seems to me mistaken. The fact that deduction guarantees soundly reasoned conclusions does not imply that it is the only way of reaching such conclusions. Making that assumption is part of the search for certainty which has bedevilled much of philosophy.[5] The assumption is at its most troublesome in moral philosophy, where so often it has seemed that what is wanted is a deductive justification for moral judgments. Such a deductive justification is impossible, though that is not to say that some moral judgments cannot be justified at all. There may be some cases where such judgments can seem to be justified by reference to a universal principle, but such principles are few, and such justifications do not take account of the complexity of moral values. In most cases we justify a moral judgment by giving reasons for it, and the right way to arrive at a moral judgment is to consider the various factors in favour of or against the action. Which of these factors is relevant to the moral judgment depends on the agent's moral values. In deciding what is the right action, an agent deliberates by considering what his values are to be, how they will apply, and even whether in the light of his assessment of the situation they need to be altered. He gives reasons for his conclusion, and may rightly claim they are adequate, even though the conclusion is not deducible.

Many candidates could be found for arguments which are good though not deductively valid. They are arguments in which the conclusion is alleged to be soundly based on its premisses: the premisses form good reasons for the conclusion, but the conclusion does not follow deductively from the premisses. One example is the argument about John's career. Another might be Betty's conclusion that she should buy a car because of the benefits of getting comfortably and safely home from work late at night. She has good reasons for her conclusion, and I can see no reason to fault it on the grounds of its not being deductive.

A Humean might suggest that these arguments must be reducible to a deductive form, that if any of these arguments were fully stated it would be seen to be deductive in form. But this is to make the point I have already dealt with in relation to suppressed premisses: it is to assume that conclusions can only be accepted on rational grounds if they follow deductively. I have found little argument to support such a point of view. Moreover the reduction of arguments to deductions can weaken them and makes them less plausible, because deductive arguments, as usually presented, are analytic, and the premisses include the conclusion within themselves. Thus it can be that a premiss which is not very plausible and which the arguer might well reject is foisted on him. Take a rather over-simplified example. Someone might argue that a particular action is wrong because it involves telling a lie. The Humean would then foist on him the principle that telling lies is always wrong, which is something he neither accepts nor needs to accept to use that argument, unless it is assumed that all arguments must be deductive.

What does the Humean say about this? His answer is again that the argument is more complex: either the premiss needs to be stated as 'Most cases of telling lies are wrong', and the conclusion adjusted to show that what was really meant was that this action was probably wrong; or the premiss must be stated so as to include clauses stating possible exceptions, and a further premiss added to the effect that this action did not come under the exceptions. The first of these methods cannot be accepted, because reformulating the argument turns it into a different argument. The agent's conclusion is that the action is wrong, and not that it is probably wrong. His conclusion may not have deductive support, but his argument may nevertheless be sound. Whether or not this is so, his real argument is not represented by supposing that he is arguing for a different conclusion from that which he states. The second method is unacceptable because at least some of those who hold that telling lies is wrong would be unwilling, and rightly unwilling, to give a complete list of exceptions. It is, they would argue, in the very nature of moral principles not to be fully determined in a way similar to that I earlier suggested for wants. The notion of *prima facie* rules or principles points in this direction, but it does not go far enough. I can consistently claim that I have an obligation to uphold the law, and also claim that on some occasions that obligation does not apply, or is overridden by another obligation—though it may not be the case that it is always overridden by the second obligation. Such obligations and the related principles are undetermined in that they do not, and cannot, specify in advance of every possible situation the way and the extent to which they apply. But this does not mean that they cannot be properly used as the basis of arguments about the rightness or wrongness of particular actions. Thus attempts to force arguments into a deductive form are to be resisted, because they provide a false account of the relation between reasons and what is concluded from them. They tend to reduce such arguments to triviality and they leave no place for judgment, a point to be defended later.

Now let us turn to the third model. It suggests that to show the deductive argument which would lead to the conclusion of the deliberation is to show what the agent is committed to. It may not be the way he argues, but it is what he must accept if he is to maintain his conclusion on good grounds. A possible ground for rejecting this model is that from the fact that a conclusion follows from certain premisses and the conclusion is accepted, it does not follow that those premisses must be accepted, since a conclusion can follow from more than one set of premises. Though this is correct, it does not do justice to the point of the argument. For in many cases in which we have a conclusion and the agent has not gone through the full process of deliberation, what we are after in trying to fill out that process is his basis for the conclusion, what it was he accepted and what would have led him to the conclusion at the time when he deliberated. We are trying to discover which of his beliefs he was committed to by his acceptance of that conclusion. However, it is a mistake to suppose that it must be something from which the conclusion can be deduced. This mistake will only be made if it is assumed that the real form of his thinking must be deductive.

My point in this and the last section is, then, that none of these models for filling out an argument show that it must be deductive, and that any of them can equally well suggest completing the argument in such a way that a different kind of reasoning is involved. The only ground for supposing that the argument has to be turned into a deductive argument is that it is assumed that nothing else is possible. I also suggest that the way an argument is completed may depend on why one wants to complete it. Interest may be directed to the justification of the conclusion, to what beliefs the arguer holds, or to the actual way he would have argued at the time if he had been more long-winded. Thus the real or logical structure of an incomplete argument may vary according to the reason why one is considering the argument. My interest in looking at deliberation follows from my interest in understanding and explaining the actions which result from that deliberation. Therefore the structure which I suggest for any actual thinking must be such as to make that thinking more intelligible—and more intelligible in a way that accords with the context of the agent's beliefs and attitudes. Someone may state the argument by which he reached a conclusion about what to do in a way which is incomplete, which is not wholly intelligible, or which leaves some uncertainties in the mind of the listener. There may be various alternative ways in which the conclusion may be rationalised. For my purposes the required rationalisation is not the one which gives the best justification for the conclusion, but rather the one which is closest to the agent's actual thinking, guessed at from his beliefs, his attitudes, his concepts, from the various things which he takes for granted in thinking. If we do this, then it is my claim that the structure need not, and often does not, take a deductive form. Moreover it is no criticism of such thinking that it does not take a deductive form.

V—*The possibility of criticism and choice*

Let me now consider two further connected difficulties in supposing that only deduction is involved in the agent's deliberation once the facts are settled. The difficulties relate to the grounds on which an agent's reasoning may be criticised, and to the way in which choice can enter into the agent's decision-making.

According to the Humean account, if an agent reaches the wrong conclusion he can only do so as a result of the inadequacy of his premises or of a mistake in his reasoning. These premises are either basic and underived or are derived from basic premises. That derivation can be included within the reasoning just mentioned. If an agent is faulted for his premises, it suggests that they could and should have been different. But these premises, insofar as they state the agent's wants, are not supported by reasons. It is just a fact about the agent that he has these wants. It is difficult to see what sense the Humean could give to the agent having chosen these wants or any other of the basic premises. If that is so, it is difficult to see on what grounds an agent could be criticised for them.

If real choice is not possible in relation to the premises of his practical reasoning, can the agent have any choice over the actual reasoning? If the reasoning is deductive then either the conclusion follows from the premises or it does not. The only alternatives for the agent when coming to a conclusion are either to draw one which validly follows, or to allege that a conclusion validly follows when it does not in fact follow. In the latter case he must be making a mistake of logic. In what circumstances can it be said that an agent can choose to make a mistake? An agent may appear to make such a choice when he does not want to reach the conclusion that the correct method of reasoning would reach. But here there must be a want, the existence of which has not been stated in the premisses, either because the agent is unwilling to recognise it, or because he is unwilling to admit it to others. Surely the only real mistakes are ones which happen by accident or unbeknown to the agent. If one is correct about one's wants, then one must want whatever follows from them and from what one believes to be the facts.[6]

Connected with the problem about choice is the problem about the possible grounds for criticising an agent's reasoning and the decision which he reaches. Of course such reasoning can be fallacious. If it is, could it be said to be a fault of the agent, unless it were the result of wilful illogicality or of negligence? I am not sure that a Humean can give a clear account of these possibilities which is consistent with the agent being blamed for them.

In many cases we disapprove of another's decision and of the way he arrived at it. We may dispute his facts; we may dispute his logic. But we may also dispute his assessment of the facts, his evaluation of the various factors, and the way he has combined these to reach a final decision.

Suppose two social workers, Angela Williams and Kenneth Carter, have to decide whether a mentally handicapped child should be admitted to an institution. They disagree about what should be done. Each might claim that they had made a responsible decision for which they could be held to account: they had reasons which justified the decision and which would enable them to criticise the alternative decision. Each might claim that, given the facts, their conclusion was inevitable. But they could criticise each other's reasoning—agreeing about the facts and not about what followed from them.

What would be the grounds of the criticism and at what point in their decision-making do they make the choices necessary for there to be responsibility? To try and settle their differences they go through the stages by which the decision was reached. They agree about the extent of the handicap, the effects on the different members of the child's family of having him at home or in the institution, the facilities and the quality of the caring at the institution, the effect of each alternative on the child's happiness and on his development. They agree that both the child's interests and the family's interests are important. Their disagreement lies in their assessment of the ways in which the interests of the child, the parents and the other children are affected and of the relative importance of the interests of each.

What account could the Humean give of the reasoning and the possible criticism of the conclusion in such a case as this? The kind of criticism expected would appear to be more than that of the basic premisses or the logical reasoning. Again neither of them would deny their responsibility for their decision and the act which might follow from it. But if that decision is deduced from basic premisses which can in no sense be chosen, how can they be responsible? Angela might claim that her conclusion was compelling and unavoidable; but this represents her view of the strength of the argument, of how good her reasons are, rather than that she had no choice in the matter.

Their disagreement is related to evaluations they make and these can be argued about. It is not just a fact about each that they make the evaluations they do; they are responsible for them, they choose them and make a commitment in doing so. In saying that the quality of caring at the institution is a reason for or against their decisions, each is allowing a ground for debate and criticism. Is it or is it not a good reason? That they do or do not take it to be a good reason is, I shall suggest, an evaluation on their part which is an essential element in their deliberation. I claim that the Humean cannot give an adequate account of this element or of the part choice plays in coming to a deliberative decision.

VI—*Complexity and conflicts*

The fourth set of difficulties with supposing the thinking in decision-making is deductive has already been touched on. It relates to the complexity of some arguments and the possible conflict between different conclusions, a conflict which has to be solved for a decision to be made. In the simplest cases of deliberation the logical reasoning rationale, even though it may not be adequate, seems to have some plausibility. But can it cope with cases where there are competing wants or desires, where the agent has to choose between alternative courses of action, each of which is supported by arguments from different desires? In such cases practical syllogisms may be constructed which have true premises and which suggest conflicting conclusions. The fact that a conclusion follows from true premises by no means shows that this conclusion must be acted on. For a simple deduction can take no account of the reasons against an action as well as the reasons in favour. It might be suggested that this is to impose too strict limits on the notion of deduction, restricting it to no more than a straightforward syllogism or *modus ponens*. Indeed this is true. But it is implicit in much of what I have argued earlier that the inadequacies of the logical account of reasoning lie not in particular accounts of deductive logic but in the very notion of deduction.

In order to clarify the issues involved here, consider an example of choosing between alternatives. Take the case of Gerald Austin who, having decided that he wants a particular kind of car, is trying to make up his mind about how to acquire it. He first dismisses without serious consideration all ways of getting the car without paying for it. These are rejected partly because they will have—or are likely to have—consequences which are undesirable, and partly because they are undesirable themselves. These methods would not even be considered by most people. Alternatives which are illegal are habitually rejected or may not even be seen as alternatives.

Gerald Austin has then decided to buy a car, and has to think about alternative ways of doing so. He can use hire-purchase, borrow money from the bank, try to win the football pools or save up the money. With the first two he gets the car at once, while with the other two he has to wait until he has got the money. The choice between the first two might, at first sight, seem to involve only a calculation of relative cost. Since he did not want to pay more than he had to, he would choose the cheaper. But the two methods may differ in other ways: they may involve different periods of time for repayment. The total cost of a shorter period of repayment may be less, but it would mean that he would have to find larger sums in the short-term, and that would be impossible without major sacrifices. The only way to raise the necessary money is to give up his nightly visit to the pub. Can he do this successfully? If so, is it worth it? Does he prefer his regular drink to paying for the car more quickly? For him to answer the last two questions may just seem to be a matter of estimating the strength of his desires or the amount of satisfaction to be got from their fulfilment.

Indeed the Humean view seems to suggest that to make a decision in such a case is just a matter of Gerald Austin observing the relative strength of his own desires, and then deducing the action that will satisfy whichever desire is strongest. Even if one is not committed to a Humean view of desires but is merely defending a deductivist view of reasoning, it is difficult to see what alternative there is to supposing that decision-making must follow a similar pattern. Let us suppose that Gerald Austin decides in favour of a three-year hire-purchase agreement, because this will not involve sacrificing his habit of visiting the pub. How, then, can a deductivist deal with such a decision?

The conclusion of the argument is that a three-year hire-purchase agreement is the best way to buy a car. The premisses are that the three-year hire-purchase agreement maximises the satisfaction of his relevant desires, and that whatever maximises the satisfaction of his desires is the best way of getting the car. The deductivist now has to give an account of how the first premiss was reached. This, he would claim, was arrived at by considering alternative courses of action and calculating the satisfaction that each produced. Gerald Austin has to predict the outcomes of the different possible actions and his reactions to those outcomes. He then has to bring together the various desires and the degree to which they are satisfied by the alternatives. He weighs up these alternatives and estimates which will produce the greater satisfaction of his desires. This might be easy if we could attach a numerical value to the degree to which each desire is satisfied, and simply compare numerical totals. Though it is not possible to do this in numerical terms such comparisons can be made by ranking the amounts of satisfaction. In complex cases this may be difficult. But I would not want to argue against the possibility of doing it. In some cases we may act on the basis of the ranking; in other cases, though the ranking does not determine the action to be done, it may nevertheless be important in coming to a decision.

Thus we have a number of elements involved in the process of reaching a decision: prediction of the consequences, prediction of the reactions of the agent to each alternative, observation of his present desires, and assessment of the relative amounts of satisfaction of them by the different alternatives. All these elements lead to the formation of a preference for that which will give greater satisfaction, and so to the actions implied by that preference. In this way decisions can be made in terms of the agent's desires by deducing a conclusion. This model suggests that even in cases of competing desires we can deduce what is the best action for the agent to do.

Let us examine this somewhat complex model of decision-making, a model which closely resembles the model embodied in decision theory.[7] Some of the reservations about this model have already been expressed, but they bear repetition in this context. Clearly a view of desires which I have argued against is implicit: estimates of degrees of satisfaction are, it is assumed, similar to predictions of how great the rainfall may be. Satisfaction is something that I just feel: the desires I have are just a fact about me. At any one time I have a certain set of desires, and any prediction about the future must suppose that I have the same kind of desires, or at least find the same things painful, pleasant, enjoyable or distasteful. Estimations of how one will be affected by various states of affairs are factual predictions about oneself. But desires do not need to be given in this way: they may be decided on by the agent. That a desire is satisfied need not be a matter of having a particular feeling, nor does the extent to which they will satisfy us provide the only grounds for trying to satisfy these desires. This model of decision-making seems to force on us a view of desires which does not apply to all that originates action. It may be the case, as I suggested in the last chapter, that some desires are of this sort, and that some conflicts between desires can be solved by finding which is the stronger in terms of present feelings or in terms of the prediction of future enjoyment. But not all desires are of this sort. Moreover, in the case of all desires except those which are compulsive, we still have the opportunity to weigh one desire against another, not by looking at their intrinsic strength, but by considering how we are to evaluate them. There are other ways of comparing desires and of deciding which desire to satisfy than by observing oneself and predicting one's reactions. Thus in order to fit in with the Humean view of deliberation such situations of conflict seem to force on us a mistaken view of desires.

VII—Possible defences of deductivism

What arguments can be used to defend the Humean view against the attack I have made on it? It may be argued, for instance, that there is a far greater variety in patterns of reasoning than I have allowed: indeed, Hare[8] and von Wright[9], among many, have been concerned to show that there are other patterns of inference than those allowed by the syllogism or by Russellian logic. I would argue that it is legitimate to widen the notion of logical reasoning to cover all reasoning which depends on purely conceptual connections. The traditional limits of logic have never been satisfactorily enshrined in a definition, and it is impossible to find any way of drawing a line between so-called logical connections and other conceptual connections. To say that one statement follows from another by logical reasoning may be taken to mean that the truth relation between them depends on the connection between the concepts employed in the two statements. If we want to see what follows from a statement, a set of statements or other kinds of expression, we have to use the links which exist between the concepts in the premisses and other concepts. It would be out of place to discuss here the different kinds of conceptual links there are, but it is important to remember that these are not confined to equivalence. Thus any arguments whose conclusion related conceptually to the premises will be an example of logical reasoning. A valid argument is one in which the conceptual link ensures that the truth of the conclusion follows from the truth of the premises.

What does this imply for the deductive account of decision-making? It implies, I think, that whatever is in the conclusion of our deliberation must be implicit in the premises. Given the premises, the conclusion of the reasoning is determined and cannot be avoided; so the decision to be made is already implicit in accepting the premises. Any conflict between desires, or more generally between feature-wants, must be solved by what is already implicit in the feature-wants referred to in the premises. Thus the action to be taken is prescribed by the feature-wants alone when applied to the particular factual situation. The feature-wants are either basic and so arrived at or formed without reasoning or they are derived from such basic feature-wants. This brings us back to the problems dealt with in the last section and reinforces the claim that to suppose deliberation is no more than logical reasoning implies a certain view of feature-wants and how feature-wants relate to making decisions. To widen the notion of deduction but still remain within the limits of conceptual connections between premises and conclusion does not help to counter my earlier arguments.

A view which might not seem to be open to my objections to deductive reasoning is that of Kenny.[10] He claims that the most important part of practical reasoning lies in a logic of satisfactoriness which applies to fiats, which, according to Kenny[11], any sentence in the optative mood is. An example of such reasoning is:

> Let me make money
> If I emigrate, I will make money
> ∴. Let me emigrate.

Arguments such as this which pass from the satisfactoriness of the first fiat to that of the conclusion do not appear to obey the rules of deduction, but nevertheless 'one and the same set of logical truths is exploited in both assertoric and practical reasoning'.[12]

Practical Reasoning

Kenny gives a sophisticated account of such reasoning. Similar in aim to it are some accounts of the structure of practical syllogisms. They may seem to provide ways of developing a deductivist view which bypasses my criticisms. I do not dispute that important points about practical reasoning come out of these discussions. But what Kenny says about his own logic of satisfactoriness is true, I think, of many of the resulting theories.

> The logic of satisfactoriness is no more than a part of practical reasoning. We have already observed that it needs to be supplemented with a logic of the description of action before it can become genuinely practical; and that in order to become an imperative logic it needs to incorporate features to take account of the difference between fiats and directives. Moreover, it fails to represent adequately something which is intuitively of great importance in practical reasoning: the weighing up of the pros and cons of a particular course of action.[13]

This weighing up with which I have been concerned seems to me to be essential to deliberation, though it is left out by accounts of deliberation which are broadly deductivist.

In the case of any decisions which go beyond the very simplest, the thinking and reasoning involved cannot merely be a matter of moving from premisses to what conceptually follows. Of course deduction can be used, as can causal reasoning when we need to discover either what will lead to a certain desire being satisfied or what are likely to be the consequences of alternative courses of action. But these are not enough.

Let me sum up the reasons for my claim that the Humean account of reasoning cannot do full justice to decision-making. Firstly, the Humean account necessitates an unsatisfactory account of desires. Secondly, it reduces deliberation to what is often relatively trivial at the expense of including what is important in the apparently non-rational premisses. Thirdly, it takes little or no account of the fact that in at least the complex cases of deliberation a decision does not follow of necessity from the wants or desires when applied to a particular situation. Decisions can be supported more or less strongly by reasons without logically following from them. Fourthly, there appears to be no way of solving the conflict that may occur between the conclusions of different deductive arguments which hold for the same situation, or at least no way of solving such conflicts rationally. Fifthly, the Humean account of what deliberation is seems to be at a far remove from the form it takes in actual practice, and no satisfactory way is suggested for bridging the gap. Sixthly, there is no room for choice and decision as they are commonly understood.

An alternative account of deliberation is thus essential and in the next chapter I shall try to provide an account which puts deliberation in its central place in decision-making.

VI
An Alternative Account of Deliberation

I—*Good reasons justify*

What is to count as deliberation? Clearly it is a kind of thinking, but it does not include the whole of thinking, let alone every activity of the mind. Day-dreaming is a form of thinking; so is contemplation. Equally the formation and application of concepts are activities of the mind. Deliberation must, then, consist of thinking in which there is an attempt to reach a conclusion and in which the conclusion is reached on the basis of the thinking. There must be a relation between the earlier stages of the deliberation and the conclusion, or at least such a relationship must be thought to exist. Random thoughts which are followed by a conclusion cannot be said to form a process of deliberation, unless, perhaps, the deliberator alleges either that there is a connection, or that forming random thoughts is a sound method of reaching correct conclusions. I confine deliberation to a movement of thought which ends with a conclusion, the grounds for which appear in the earlier stages of the thinking.

If my account is to compete with the Humean account it would seem that one further condition needs to be satisfied. It must be possible to distinguish between the form of the deliberation and its subject matter, so that each can be assessed independently of the other. It must be possible to say of any deliberation that in it the agent has reasoned well or poorly: there must be standards of reasoning to which he either conforms or fails to conform. Such standards are—in the case of deduction—objective, and any example of reasoning can be tested independently of the subject matter. Thus it seems that the assessment of any piece of deliberation should be independent of the assessment of the beliefs, tastes or values of the deliberator; in so far as such beliefs and values affect the conclusion they are included in the premisses. It is the desirability of such objective standards which gives plausibility to the argument that all reasoning should be reduced to deductive reasoning. Such a reduction, it is claimed, reveals the different elements in any piece of deliberation, and separates what is subjective from what is objective.

This is an important point. An account of deliberation is unacceptable if it allows complete freedom to the reasoner in the way he reasons; if it allows that anyone has reasoned correctly if he claims that he has, irrespective of how his conclusions were reached; or if it allows the method of reasoning used to become simply a matter of personal preference. However, I shall argue in due course that the standards for deliberation cannot always be given in ways which allow any piece of deliberation to be tested by a standard procedure. It is not always possible to separate the form and the subject matter of the deliberation. But the importance of finding legitimate methods of criticising any piece of reasoning must be accepted. Thus in this chapter I shall try to give an account of the process by which agents legitimately reach conclusions about what to do, and which allows their reasoning to be evaluated even if not only by reference to principles of logic.

Let me try to summarise this alternative account. In any reasoning the conclusion is supported by reasons: the relation of the reasons to the conclusion may be deductive but it does not need to be. I can make a claim, and I can defend that claim by pointing to the reasons on which I based it; I can enter into a debate both about what is asserted within the reasons and about how far that content provides a good reason for my conclusion. Such a debate is not about whether the conclusion follows from the reasons by necessity: deductive certainty is far rarer in reasoning than works of logic seem to indicate. Good reasons can be distinguished from bad reasons and thus some conclusions, but not others, are justified. This approach has been used in ethics by Baier and others,[1] but has not been applied to the problems of explanation so often.

Suppose someone has a problem about what to do. He begins by considering the context, by looking at all the facts he considers relevant. To do this he may have to make predictions about what might happen, predictions which cannot be based solely on induction or arrived at by the application of well-treated generalisations. He has to use his judgment, something for which everyone has a capacity to a greater or lesser degree, though that capacity may vary according to the particular field in which it is to be applied. In addition he has to evaluate the various factors which might support the alternative solutions, not simply for their effectiveness in bringing about a desired end, but for their intrinsic desirability. He has to decide what is to count as a reason, and what is to count as a *good* reason. These reasons are given weight, and after relating the different reasons to each other the agent has to decide which solution to the problem is supported with sufficient reasons or with the strongest reasons.

In making a decision about what is to count as a reason for him, the agent is not deciding about what is the case, but about what is to be the case. It is not like deciding about a matter of fact, for instance whether there are more or less than ten people in the room. Rather it is through his decision that it is a reason for him. In making that decision he is evaluating and committing himself to a particular evaluation.

According to my view a good deliberator or reasoner is not someone who simply obeys the rules of logic, but someone who is also a sound judge and can defend his decisions about how to act by pointing to reasons which support them. The deductivist tries to reduce the elements of sound judgment and correct evaluation either to the application of logic or to a kind of subjective response. He may claim that a view such as mine downgrades the importance of reason by lessening the importance of logic. But rather than downgrading it I am trying to show that reason—though it may not always be clear-cut and uncontroversial in its application as the deductivist would suggest—is far wider in its significance, and has a far more important role in action, than might appear from the deductivist account.

II—Comparisons

In order to develop this idea of deliberation I want to begin by examining the way comparisons are made. Comparing is, firstly, an important kind of thinking towards a conclusion which can give a right answer, though not necessarily one which is deduced. Secondly, it bears a close relation to evaluating.

We compare two objects or two activities in respect of a shared characteristic which each may have to a different degree. Is this stone heavier than that one? Is this book longer than the other? Is this route quicker than the alternative one? Is Miles more efficient than Hugh? Amongst the simplest comparisons are those of characteristics which are immediately observable like the roughness of a texture or the loudness of a sound. Again any comparison reducible to numerical terms is simple and can be settled without controversy. Not all the criteria for the making of comparisons are precise, and this is not necessarily a disadvantage: Is Hugh balder than Miles? Is this field marshier than that one? Some characteristics cannot be measured, and so no numerical comparison is possible with these. Moreover where there is such a criterion it is not always possible to apply it.

What of the thinking involved in such comparisons? At first the simple comparisons may seem to involve nothing more than the immediate observation of perceptible properties. But this is not so. We can perceive the characteristics of two objects without making a comparison. I see that this object has a certain colour; I also see that a second object has a second colour. I need be in no doubt as to what I have seen or what their colours are, without having to draw the conclusion that the one is darker than the other. If we were not able to make comparisons our powers of discrimination might be small and our ability to state what we perceive might be curtailed. But this does not mean that comparisons involve nothing but the perception of the objects being compared. I would suggest that even the simplest comparison involves thinking, and the statement of how two objects compare is a conclusion reached by thinking about the perception of them. It is tempting to argue that such a

An Alternative Account of Deliberation 77

simple comparison is not a deduction; but though on the whole this is true, I do not think the simple cases provide the crucial examples.

Consider two simple comparisons: the width of two doorways, and the dryness of two wines. In the former the widths are measurable, and the comparison is reducible to which of two numbers is the larger. If one doorway is one metre wide, and the other doorway is two metres wide, then it follows that the second is larger than the first. The conclusion is surely deductively valid, whether or not it conforms to a typical deductive pattern. In the comparison of the two wines, the conclusion is that one wine is drier than the other, and it is difficult to see how the conclusion could be said to have been reached deductively. In practice the conclusion would be defended by the two wines being tasted again or by others, or by making comparisons with other wines where there is no disagreement. Indicating the dryness of each wine provides sufficient reasons for our conclusions.

Consider another more complex example. Suppose Antony Arbuckle is giving advice about driving from A to B and has to consider two different routes. There are many factors which might affect his advice, such as places of historical interest or the attractiveness of the scenery. Let us suppose that it is only the time taken which is to determine the choice of route. Times for past journeys may not be available, and even if they were, they would only relate to the time taken under certain conditions. In practice he would rely on a variety of information about the routes, such as their straightness, difficult junctions, traffic congestion, road works, or the time the journey took on other occasions, and the extent to which conditions then were typical and gave reliable information about future journeys. He would have to bring together these different elements, considering each route in relation to each factor. As a result a judgment is formed about which route would be the quicker. This judgment is the conclusion of a piece of reasoning which cannot be deduced, but which can be either well or poorly supported. This judgment may or may not turn out to be correct, but this is not necessarily an indication of the adequacy of the reasoning. On the evidence available to Antony, his conclusion may have been correct, and yet there may have been factors, which were unknown to him and which no one could have been expected to know, that made his judgment wrong.

There are various ways in which someone might try to reduce this piece of reasoning to a deduction. Firstly, it might be suggested that there must be a principle, whether it is held explicitly or implicitly, which guides the way the various elements are to be combined into a final judgment. But what form could such a principle take? Could any such principle guarantee that the answer suggested by it was the one justified by the evidence? Would it not be more like a rule of thumb which guides us to, but does not justify the answer? The way in which the principle should be applied would not always be clear-cut, and if it were applied as a matter of routine would often be open to criticism. Reasons could be given for suggesting that the answer arrived at was wrong. If frequently engaged in planning routes without, perhaps, a great deal of time to spare, then Antony Arbuckle might work out a rough principle which would give a starting point for getting an answer. It might even in some cases be the sole basis for his conclusion, even though he knows that more time and thought might provide a better one. Alternatively he might have a method of working out approximate times for routes, allowing for different speeds on different types of roads and a fixed number of minutes for different types of hazard. In many cases such a method would allow a simple calculation of times for different routes and a comparative conclusion could then be deduced. But it could prove inadequate for particular cases. The allowance would be rough and ready and could not take account of all differences.

A more sophisticated principle could be formulated, and in some cases where the elements to be combined are constant and measurable it might work. We might try and test different possibilities against the skills of various route-planners who did not use such a principle. When tested against their judgment the principles might give a better answer because the route-planners were bad judges. Just as machines can turn out a standard product more economically and better than most craftsmen, and can turn out a non-standard product less well than a good craftsman though better than a bad craftsman, so it is with such a principle. In some cases it will work best; in other cases it will work less well than the judgment of all but the worst of route-planners. However, the way in which a principle is to be applied in particular circumstances does not follow automatically from accepting it in general terms. Reasoning not only would have to be used to formulate and defend the principle, it would also have to be used in deciding how it applied to particular cases—for instance did hedge-cutting count as a road work? Such reasoning would not be deductive. It might be suggested that a computer could solve the problem. Certainly the use of a computer would allow for greater complexity than any principle, and the basis for its calculations might seem to be deductive. Though I cannot say more about the computer model for deliberation[2] here, there are two points that need to be made. Firstly, just as reasoning is required to formulate a principle, so it is required for the construction of the computer-programme, and the same doubts about such reasoning being deductive occur. Secondly, a computer-programme is based on past information and is therefore not capable of dealing with novel and unexpected aspects of a new situation. Hence, though a computer may be more efficient on the whole, it is not able to represent the full range of thinking in which an individual may engage.

Thus deduction alone will rarely give the solution to such a problem. But that does not imply the absence of reason. The procedures used in arriving at such a solution are rational because the solution is found by making comparisons of the facts, and because reasons could be given in defence of the conclusion. We can argue about the conclusion, suggesting for instance that insufficient attention has been given to the fact that the narrowness of one road may result in delays if there is other traffic. Though it is unlikely to be worth extended argument, there certainly could be such argument, and it might help to get a better answer.

Consider another comparison. Suppose we are interested in the productiveness of two varieties of apple tree. Such a comparison, though still at least partly factual, may also involve an evaluative element. The one variety gives a great many apples which are small; the other gives somewhat fewer apples of a larger size. Two people may give different answers to the comparison. Robert Sturmer suggests that the first is more productive because the total weight produced is greater. On the other hand, Donald Cox argues that total weight is not in itself decisive, and that a bigger size of apple may compensate for a slightly smaller total weight, so that the second is the more productive. Now this disagreement may be alleged to depend on Robert and Donald holding different ideas of what counts as productiveness. Each applies a standard and deduces a conclusion. If agreement about the standard is achieved then all we need to do is to make certain measurements of weight and deduce the conclusion. Several points need to be made about this. Firstly, Donald Cox might come to his conclusion without being able or willing to enshrine his standard in a principle. He might think both weight and size important without wanting to lay down a principle relating their importance in exact proportions. The argument would then not be about a principle but would rather be about how strong were the different reasons for saying that a variety was productive. Donald might ask why size was important as well as weight and reasons might be given. Equally—and this takes us to the second point—even though Donald, as well as Robert, applied a principle, the two principles would be a matter for debate and would be supported with reasons. At this point the argument becomes one about questions which are partially evaluative. The disagreement over principles is a disagreement about the appropriate standard for productiveness, and this to some extent will be about what kinds of apple are desirable. There may be cases in which the choice of an appropriate standard seems to be settled by reference to the facts, but even in these cases it is more appearance than reality. I shall return to the question of evaluation later. The only point I want to make now is that an appeal to principles is not necessary, and even

An Alternative Account of Deliberation 81

where it occurs it does not automatically remove the need for non-deductive reasons.

In considering these comparisons we have to raise the question of how far we can apply standards to the thinking which has led to the conclusion, how far we can say that someone has reached his comparative judgment as a result of good or bad reasoning. It may be possible to ascertain whether such a judgment is true, whether one route is quicker than another by travelling the two routes under a variety of conditions. But, as in a deductive argument, the truth of the conclusion does not show that the reasoning must have been sound. No doubt if Antony Arbuckle hazarded a guess or only calculated the length of the two routes we would think his procedures inadequate, even though he had got the right answer. On the other hand if he had examined and assessed each route very carefully, and yet was wrong about the relative quickness of the two routes, we might nevertheless agree that his reasoning was sound. But a careful examination is not in itself enough; his reasoning might be attacked either by pointing out a factor which he has wholly neglected, or by suggesting that though the right factors have been considered and given the appropriate weight, yet nevertheless the final judgment is wrong since the way the different factors are combined together was mistaken. In practice it is difficult to separate the different ways of attacking a comparison and it is especially difficult to decide whether what is at fault is the way the factors have been weighted or is the way the factors have been combined.

My argument, then, is that in factual comparisons reasoning occurs and cannot always be reduced to deduction. Reasons can be given for the comparative conclusion, and they can support it though they need not logically imply it. In some cases the conclusion is obvious, though it may not always be reached because some people have poorer powers of judgment than others and thus are less likely to reach the right conclusion. In other cases there is no one conclusion which on available evidence is clearly correct; different people who have equallly good powers of judgment may arrive at different conclusions. The evidence for or against the use of chemical fertilisers in horticulture may give more or less the same degree of support to each conclusion, though different people—all with good judgment—passionately advance opposing conclusions. Both conclusions may be challenged. Each is attacked by pointing out the inadequacy of the reasons for that conclusion and the neglect of certain reasons against it; each is defended by pointing out the reasons which support that conclusion and by arguing for their superiority over the reasons against. It is not the case that there must be a deduction which can be tested for logical error, and that, if not, there can be no reasoning which can be subjected to criticism and can be judged good or bad.

III—*Evaluative comparisons*

I shall now extend this account of comparisons to those which result in what looks like an evaluative conclusion of the form 'This is the best X'. I want to start with comparisons which are closest to being factual, where the criterion for the best X is in factual terms and is generally accepted. The most straight-forward case is where the subjects of the comparison have been designed for a purpose, and the comparison depends on the extent to which the purpose is achieved. A decision about which of two tin-openers is the best will almost always be made in terms of their relative efficiency at opening tins. The best stain-remover will in almost all cases be determined by how well stains are removed. In both cases empirical tests can be made, and thus for all practical purposes they are factual comparisons. It is possible that other more debatable characteristics might be introduced such as the attractiveness of the tin-openers or the unpleasantness of the smell of the stain-remover, but for the most part the criteria for the comparisons are factual and agreed.

There are other comparisons where the criteria may not be so obvious, but where within a particular group or society there is so much agreement that the comparison can be settled factually. There may be disagreement with other

An Alternative Account of Deliberation 83

groups because of differing needs or purposes, thus making debate about a comparison pointless. For instance the best hour-glass may at one period have been the one most efficient at estimating an hour, while now it may be judged on aesthetic grounds. Yachtsmen and gymnasts use ropes for different purposes, and will thus decide on the best rope by different criteria. For each, that decision can be made by settling matters of fact. To cases of this type, the account of the last section applies.

There are contrasting examples where the criteria may not be agreed, they may be a matter for debate, or they may be a matter of individual judgment or taste. In such cases neither the object being compared nor the context of the comparison makes the criteria clear. In considering the best method of electricity generation for the future, not only efficiency and cost, but also dangers to health and the effect on the landscape may be considered. There are strong and differing views about the extent to which the avoidance of possible dangers to health should be sacrificed for increased efficiency and reduced cost, and thus about the criteria for the best method of electricity generation.

Less emotionally charged examples of evaluative comparisons occur when Mary Casson, who is a careers adviser, tries to suggest the best job for different individuals and bases her advice on each individual's tastes, values and abilities. She will have to make a number of factual comparisons, such as the pay prospects of different careers. Having made comparisons in relation to the various factors, she then has to reach an over-all comparison. Occasionally only one factor might be relevant, but in most cases a number of factors will have to be related to each other. It is possible that there are rules by which the evaluations of the different factors can be compounded. If so, the application of the rule may be a straightforward matter of calculation. For that to be the case, pay must always be rated against security in the same way irrespective of particular circumstances; if the rule is not so precise, then its application will be much less straightforward. However, in cases like these it is rare for there to be a rule, even one that is less precise; the same situation does not often recur, different situations do not have enough in common and one's reactions to those situations are not similar enough for a rule to be of much use. In practice what happens is that we either arrive at the judgment without a rule, or use the rule as a starting point and adjust the judgment it suggests according to the particular circumstances. But it is both possible and legitimate to make such a judgment without using a rule.

Let us consider a little further what is involved in making these judgments without the help of rules. In determining which job would be best for Kevin Granger, Mary Casson first finds out about his abilities and interests. In the light of this information she tries to list the various conditions which would have to be satisfied by an acceptable career, and after discussion decides how important each condition is. She considers possible careers and the degree to which each satisfies the conditions. Thus she may decide that one job is more exciting, while another is more secure; excitement is a reason for choosing the first and security for choosing the second. From weighing up these reasons, she comes to a final judgment, a judgment supported by reasons.

There are two decisions to be made in relation to any factor. Firstly, a decision is required about how different jobs rate in relation to that factor. Secondly, a decision is required about the importance of the factor relative to other factors. The first decision only involves comparisons of a factual kind. The second involves comparisons which depend on the tastes, interests or values of the judge or of the person for whom the decision is to be made. Though the conclusion finally reached depends on the relative importance of each factor, this does not imply that either a principle is being employed or, if not, that there is no reasoning involved. It is true that some moralists pay great homage to moral principles, but as I shall argue in Chapter VIII there is much to be said against their view. Even if one did have such principles they still have to be related to each other, and the only way that can be done without bringing in something other than principles is by having one ultimate principle, or a fixed order of priority for principles; both these methods raise well-known difficulties.[3] My argument here is limited to the claim that it is possible to make over-all comparisons by reasoning but without reference to rules, and that in some cases such a method provides a better representation of what does and should happen in making comparisons than any rules could provide.

Suppose Mary Casson comes to the conclusion that the best job for Kevin is journalism. She may do so by constructing an argument similar to one she might use to defend her conclusion against criticism. She has discovered that he has skills in writing and dealing with people and that he enjoys an outdoor life which provides excitement. He would prefer a job near home and is more concerned about security than the possibility of high pay. No job will meet all these demands, but the reasons in favour of journalism seem to outweigh those against, more than they do for other possible jobs. A colleague present at the interviews suggests that she gave too little weight to Kevin's wanting to live near home, which is unlikely to be possible in journalism. She defends herself by saying that in her judgment this was something temporary, which results from the insecurity of leaving school and having to make long-term decisions.

Mary eliminates all but two possibilities—journalism and local government—in her search for the best job for Kevin. In each of these she finds a number of features which in the light of Kevin's abilities and interests suggest either would be a good career for him. These features give reasons in favour of that career. Equally there will be a number of features of each career suggesting that it is unsuitable. These provide reasons against. She then has to compare the reasons for and against each, and decide which is the more strongly supported. Thus the form of the reasoning is:

P, Q and R are reasons in favour of journalism being the best career
S, T and U are reasons against journalism being the best career
P, Q and R outweigh S, T and U
Therefore journalism is the best career.

It would be difficult to deny that this argument is deductive. Where, then, is the non-deductive reasoning? My claim is that it is involved in the formation of the premises and this is the most important reasoning. To arrive at the view that P is a reason in favour of journalism involves deliberation, and so does deciding that the reasons in favour of journalism outweigh those against. I, therefore, want to examine two types of statement. P is a reason for J and P is a stronger reason than Q for J.

The deductivist claims that the argument from P—journalism provides excitement—to J—journalism is the best career for Kevin—must be deductive and thus an additional premiss must be added. It is not easy to see what that premiss should be; but leaving that aside, completing the argument so that it is valid (Chapter V, Section II) does not necessarily represent what is being argued. Without completing it in this way, P cannot be a conclusive reason for J; either it is not a reason at all or it is a good reason which is not conclusive.

What makes a reason a good reason if it is not a deductive reason? Clearly a good reason supports a conclusion without giving deductive support. How then do we tell whether a reason gives that support? It is impossible to give any general criterion for what makes a good reason. In the case under consideration here, and I take it to be typical, clearly the criterion involves evaluations and agreement on P being a good reason for J will depend on shared evaluations. These are not necessarily of a moral type, and do not need to be general. There is no difference between saying P is a good reason for J, and saying that P is evaluated highly in relation to J. This is not to suggest that reason-statements require evaluative principles as premisses. It is rather that they are, or express, evaluations, which though they can be general, are most often particular.

Though not the conclusions of a deduction, reason-statements can be defended and given reasons in the same way as they provide reasons for the statements they support. In almost all cases it is legitimate to ask of a reason on what grounds it is a reason. This is not to deny that there are some occasions when a reason does not require justification: if the reason for an action is that it avoids unnecessary and useless pain, then that reason surely requires no defence and it would be difficult to understand what was in the mind of anyone who challenged it.

If a deductive account cannot be given of 'P is a reason for J', the same must be true of 'P is a stronger reason for J than Q is'. Indeed it seems difficult to give any account of the rationality of this last statement in deductivist terms. Again I want to say that it expresses an evaluation and that it is open to challenge: there can be non-deductive reasons for it. 'P is a reason for J' is an evaluation of P in relation to J; 'P is a stronger reason than Q for J' is an evaluation of P in relation to J relative to other reasons for or against J.

Are objective standards possible for these kinds of evaluative deliberations? In the factual case there is a method of testing the deliberation by seeing how far the answers arrived at turn out to be correct. In the present cases it is more difficult. Someone may, after being challenged, admit that he has made a mistake. He may go over the steps of his deliberation, and while not revising his factual claims see that a different conclusion is required. He may change what he thinks are reasons, or how highly he rates his reasons; or he may realise that even with his judgments of reasons unchanged, nevertheless the way he put these together to reach a conclusion is unsatisfactory. In practice it is difficult to show which particular aspect of any reasoning is at fault, whether it is the evaluative or the non-evaluative parts which need to be corrected.

Consider again Mary Casson's deliberation about whether journalism or local government is the better career for Kevin. Journalism is better because it gives a certain amount of excitement and uses his writing skills, while local government provides a job near home with security. Mary might be challenged on the grounds that the amount of excitement in journalism is not likely to be great and the difference in the way the two careers use his writing skills is small, while there is a considerable difference between them as regards the other two characteristics. Therefore she must have combined her original reasons in the wrong way and come to the wrong conclusion. She might admit she had made a mistake and that her reasons when taken together support a different conclusion. Alternatively she could defend herself by indicating the greater importance attached to the reasons which support journalism. It may be pointed out that on other occasions she thought excitement less important than security even for people similar to Kevin. She may admit to a change of mind or, more significantly, claim that Kevin's particular circumstances do make a great difference. The importance of a factor clearly need not be constant, but may, with consistency, be held to vary according to other factors in the situation. The critic cannot easily tell whether Mary has made a mistake in her reasons or in how she reaches a conclusion from them but she can admit to the possibility of a mistake. In all deliberation, there is always such a possibility and a deliberator may revise his conclusion by going over his reasoning even though he does not change any of the particular judgments in it.

My argument about objective standards is that, apart from logical principles, there are no principles to which we can appeal in assessing the way someone has deliberated. Nor do I think that logical principles get us very far in making such assessments, though I am not suggesting that it is right to contravene such principles. The idea that logic is the sole basis for such assessments leads, in my view, to a devaluation of reasoning and the ways it can be criticised. Though it may not be possible to lay down general statements about what counts as a good or bad reason for criticising an argument, nevertheless, as these are open to the challenge of debate, we can develop the ability to deliberate better and to assess deliberation. Thus in a particular context a reason for criticising a piece of deliberation may be objective even though not based on a principle of logic: its objectivity lies in its being open to challenge and in its ability to withstand criticism. This may not be the degree of objectivity that some would think desirable, but I think it is enough for deliberation to be said to be reasoning and not caprice. If I have understood Habermas rightly, then my suggestion about objectivity here is close to his account of the way in which the social sciences require—and have—objectivity.[4]

IV—Decision-making

It is a small step from evaluative comparisons of the type just discussed to decisions about how to act. Many such decisions may seem to be decisions about what is the best thing to do. There are cases where there does seem to be a gap between comparisons and decisions—a gap analogous to that between liking and wanting. To believe that this is the best car and not choose it may be puzzling, but is certainly possible, just as it is possible to like something without wanting it. The comparative judgment and having a liking do not demand action, though they may make it natural for it to follow, while the decision about how to act and having a feature-want have a far stronger connection with action. If the agent does not act on his decision, then either he was unable to do so or he revised his decision.

Let me return to the case of Thomas Fagg (Chapter II, Section II) who is trying to decide whether to give up smoking, and use that example to summarize my points about deliberation in decision-making. In deliberating he considers the various factors relevant to his decision: the effect on his health, the pleasure smoking gives him and the beneficial effect which smoking has on his work and on his ability to get on with others. He determines as best he can how each of these factors would affect him, evaluates them, and thus forms a feature-want, which gives him a reason for or against smoking. But making such evaluations without relating them to each other is no more than the first stage, even though without it the decision-making process might not get started. What he additionally needs to do is to evaluate the factors in relation to each other and in so doing to evaluate his feature-wants in relation to each other. It is one thing to form an evaluation of a factor independently of its context, quite another to evaluate it in relation to all the relevant factors when they are set against each other. Thomas Fagg may decide that he wants to be healthy, but he still has to make a further judgment of how much he wants it when he considers this want in the context of the other wants relevant to his decision. His evaluation of this factor in the context of the deliberation is not implied by his evaluation of it when taken on its own, unless it is assumed that the value of each factor is fixed and unchanging irrespective of context. It is difficult to see why this should be assumed. Sometimes health considerations may be absolutely overriding for Thomas Fagg: in another situation because of other factors they might be much less important. Contrary to appearances, the different status of health considerations in different situations does not imply a change in values. He can make a judgment about the importance generally of health considerations and he can make another similar judgment about his enjoyment of smoking. But a further judgment is required when the two have to be combined. As the former judgment is combined with the different judgments required by the presence of different factors, so a different emphasis may be placed on good health. A conclusion goes beyond the evaluation of particular factors and thus involves an evaluation which does not follow from other evaluations already made.

As with comparisons this may be put in terms of reasons. In a situation requiring a decision, we have first to decide what factors are *prima facie* reasons, that is what factors need to be considered to see whether they provide reasons for or against any of the alternatives. We then have to decide which *prima facie* reasons are in fact reasons. This is the first stage of the evaluation. After that we have to weigh up these reasons, consider them in the light of each other and reach a conclusion, and this again is an evaluation. The conclusion can be defended by pointing to the factors which were thought to be most important: these constituted the reasons why the action was performed. We might go further and try to indicate what it was about each of these factors which made us give them weight, thus giving grounds for claiming that the factors constituted reasons for the action.

Implicit in what I say is a view of what is involved in evaluating. It is not just having and noticing a feeling, an emotion, or anything which is merely an immediate response: it requires thought, though not deductive reasoning. Evaluating is not a passive reaction, but is rather a form of thoughtful activity. An agent has to decide on the value which factors or actions are to have, and in so doing he is giving them that value: he chooses the value they are to have. It is not an arbitrary choice, but one in which, if it is to be done properly, the evaluator must think about what he is doing. He is commiting himself to the value judgment and is claiming that it is his judgment: it belongs to him and he bears responsibility for it.

So in determining that a factor is to constitute a reason and a sufficient reason the agent is making this commitment, and the whole process of deliberating can be a complex pattern of evaluation and factual discovery. The conclusion cannot follow deductively from premises and cannot, as in deduction, be contained within the premises, because this does not allow for the element of determination by the agent. He cannot start with a set of feature-wants and from those and the facts alone arrive at a conclusion. Even where his feature-wants are not the result of his evaluation but are caused, they can—indeed they must if the action is to be deliberative—remain to some extent undetermined, only becoming settled within the particular context.

My argument is that an agent comes to a decision about what to do by recognising that certain factors may be relevant, by deciding that these factors constitute reasons to be taken account of in any decision about what to do, and then by weighing these against each other. Thus not only has a decision to be made about whether a factor constitutes a reason, but also a decision is required about how important each reason is in the light of all the reasons relevant to the situation.

V—The process of deliberation

Let me try to draw together the threads of my argument about the nature of deliberation. Deliberation starts from a problem which may be about what made this event happen or what its consequences are likely to be; the attempt to solve such a problem belongs to theoretical deliberation, which I have only been marginally concerned with. On the other hand the problem may be about what action will best achieve a given end or about which of several alternatives should be chosen. To think about such problems with a view to coming to a conclusion about what is to be done is to engage in practical deliberation.

Such deliberation may involve thinking about what is relevant to the problem, finding possible solutions, working out the ways in which each solution can be supported and thus what are possible reasons for each, and deciding what weight the different reasons should have. In some cases practical deliberation may reduce to theoretical deliberation about the means to a given end; but this reduction may be more apparent than real, since a means to a given end is likely to have other consequences and those consequences need to be considered and balanced against the desired end.

In all deliberation—whether practical or theoretical—the basic move is from one statement to another for which the first is a good reason. There are a variety of ways in which one statement, P, may be a good reason for another, Q. It may be that Q can be deduced from P and then P is a conclusive reason for Q. However this is not the only way P can be a good reason for Q. P may provide evidence for Q, though not indubitable or unchallengeable evidence. Reasons can be good and sufficient to justify a conclusion without being deductive. Indeed in the context of deliberation reasons which are not deductive are the most important.

Whether P is a good reason for Q is a matter of whether the truth of P makes the truth of Q more likely, of whether it provides evidence or support for Q. Where the deliberation is theoretical, factual information will provide such support. Where the deliberation is practical, such support depends on evaluation. To come to a conclusion about what to do on the basis of reasons depends on the evaluation of the factors which are candidates for being reasons. Such evaluation can occur in the formation of feature-wants or in the consideration of the feature-wants already held. The process of deliberation includes evaluation as a form of thinking, relating the separate evaluations to each other and weighing up the reasons for and against a conclusion.

Is it possible to separate the evaluations or the evaluating from the reasoning? I do not think so. In deliberating we cannot first state our values and then reason about them: the two activities are inextricably mixed up. We evaluate in the process of forming reasons and in the process of relating different reasons to each other. Our evaluations are often shown by the way we reason. This may seem to indicate that an agent's reasoning cannot be assessed independently of his evaluations and that whatever his values are he has reasoned inadequately. But this is not so. An observer can claim that a deliberator omitted any consideration of certain factors which are relevant even in terms of his own values, was unable to deal with the complexity of the reasons and was unable to see the reasons in relation to each other. Or the deliberator may be alleged to have forgotten certain feature-wants which were relevant when considering another feature-want, or to have been inconsistent in the weight he gave to different reasons when coming to a conclusion. These are examples of the kinds of criticism of reasoning which can be made. They suggest a point of great importance, that there are ways in which people can reason better without having to pay more attention to the laws of logic, and by reflecting on their deliberation can make it more comprehensive and consistent.

VII
Action

I—Deliberation and feature-wants
The point of practical deliberation is to 'arrive at a decision' about what to do and then to act on that decision. But to decide is one thing and to act is another. How do we get from a decision, represented by the conclusion of a deliberation to action? Clearly there are times when we do not act on our decisions, the clearest examples being those which show weakness of will. In this chapter I shall discuss how this gap between decision and action is to be filled. To do so it is first necessary to say more about the way feature-wants can arise from deliberation and can be the subject of it.

Jack and Jill are told the unhappy stories of two children, Jeremy and Joanna, who need a foster parent. Jack reacts immediately and wants to foster Jeremy. He feels an impulse to do so which is immediate and not in any way the result of deliberation, but is more like a response to a stimulus. Jill feels sorry for Joanna and would like to see her helped, but is not sure whether she wants to foster her; she thinks she needs to give much more thought to the situation before deciding what she wants. After she has given it thought she decides that she does want to foster Joanna. Both Jack and Jill have a feature-want directed towards a similar feature, but each is formed in a different way. For Jack there is no deliberation: he responds immediately and the feature-want may therefore be said to have been caused by his hearing about Joanna and will thus be an impulse-desire, as defined in Chapter IV, Section I. For Jill, on the other hand, there is a process of weighing up advantages and disadvantages, as a result of which she arrives at a conclusion about what she wants in relation to fostering. In the light of both of their differing wants about this and of their other wants, each of them then tries to make up his or her mind about what to do. In the end they both decide to offer themselves as foster-parents.

The following points need discussion. Firstly, what is the nature of Jill's alleged deliberation about whether or not she wants to foster Joanna. Secondly, can Jack's and Jill's alleged feature-wants both be legitimately said to be feature-wants, and if they can are they feature-wants of the same kind? Thirdly, how do they get from their feature-wants to the conclusion of their deliberation?

If, at the time she hears about Joanna, Jill is asked whether or not she wants to foster her, she will reply that she does not know. She could try to make up her mind in one of two ways. One of these is by deciding what her reactions to fostering the child would be. She tries to become clearer about what it would be like to foster her, and when she is clearer, asks herself what she would feel in that situation, and what she now feels. Once she understands more fully what it is she is to respond to she can ask herself whether or not she wants to foster. She is observing her own responses—responses of the same kind as Jack's impulse-desire, except that she takes trouble to find out more about what she should be responding to. Her feature-want is an impulse-desire, though one only formed after factual deliberation.

However, this is not Jill's approach. She makes up her mind in a different way and uses a different kind of deliberation in order to decide what she wants. She considers the various aspects of the situation and decides how important each is, thus evaluating rather than responding directly. The helping of a child in need is obviously desirable and she thinks she could help. But if she took on Joanna she would have to give up some of her drama work with a group of disturbed adolescents, as well as her own acting which she enjoys very much. By evaluating these factors she forms a feature-want directed towards each relevant aspect. Of course there are some features of fostering to which she cannot help responding emotionally—children who answer back make her angry. Thus she will have impulse-desires as well as deliberative feature-wants and all of these have to be evaluated in relation to each other. How important is her anger when weighed against the security she can give the child? She is asking herself for reasons both for and against wanting to foster. Having a certain immediate response to some aspect may or may not be a reason; that is something she must decide. She weighs up the advantages and disadvantages, evaluating various factors and as a result comes to a decision that she wants to foster. This final decision is not something caused—her feature-want is not an impulse-desire. She has deliberated about what her feature-want is to be, and justifies her conclusion rather than verifying that having the feature-want is her response to the situation.

Are the ways in which Jack and Jill form their feature-wants consistent with the conditions I laid down for feature-wants (Chapter III, Sections III and IV)? Clearly both their feature-wants have an object—fostering—and that object is a possible feature of a future state of affairs. They each seem to have a pro-attitude towards the feature, and it is reasonable to suppose that in the absence of conflicting feature-wants they are motivated to foster. Indeed if they were not so motivated, not only would they not have a feature-want, they could not even be said to want to foster. But to deal with the question of motivation, it is necessary to look further at the way they deliberate about their feature-wants.

Jack's and Jill's feature-wants are not compulsive, and therefore they can consider whether or not to satisfy them. In most cases they will have to decide about the relative importance of their feature-wants towards fostering compared with others they may have. It is possible that this is the only feature-want they have, but that does not make it impossible for them to form other feature-wants. Deliberation is not only possible when there are several competing wants, but may also be undertaken in order to decide whether there are features, other than the one already wanted, which should be wanted. In Jack's case he can consider other features which fostering the child would have. As a result he can, if he so decides, form feature-wants and compare them with the original one. Thus it is not the case that someone must automatically act on a feature-want if it is the only one he has. Though Jack has no other feature-wants to begin with, he can start to think about the effects of a foster-child on his own children, his unwillingness to give the extra help that would be needed, or the financial costs of fostering. As a result he may or may not form feature-wants in relation to these. If he does not and believes that there are no other features to be considered, then he has decided to give effect to the original feature-want. If he does form other feature-wants then he has to decide how much weight to give to each of the feature-wants he finally has. As a result of such an evaluation of his feature-wants he reaches a decision.

Jill's case is somewhat different. In forming her feature-want towards fostering, she has already considered other features and evaluated them as providing reasons for and against fostering. Thus rather than being a first stage of her deliberation, forming the feature-want towards fostering represents the end of her deliberation, in which she decides what she wants to do. Nevertheless, it would be possible to see part of her deliberation as the forming of feature-wants, and part as the comparing of these with each other and with any impulse-desires she has. It is necessary for her to evaluate features to which she is favourably inclined, even though she does not explicitly form the feature-want.

I thus want to argue that in the case of Jack and Jill deliberation can involve forming feature-wants or evaluating feature-wants. If this is an acceptable interpretation, then it shows that these are possibilities in any deliberation. Indeed, without feature-wants being either formed or evaluated or both an action would not be voluntary. Thus an agent can have feature-wants which are impulse-desires or are deliberative, that is, arrived at through deliberation. An agent can evaluate his feature-wants, and may or may not be able to give effect to the results of that evaluation. But his action, if intentional, is the putting into effect of his concluding or dominant feature-want.

II—*Closing the gap between reasoning and action*
I have shown how deliberation can reach its conclusion. How is that conclusion related to the resulting action? Does action result automatically, or must there be something like an act of will by which the agent transforms the conclusion into an action? To suppose it is automatic fails to take

account of the gap there can be between reaching a conclusion and acting. Sometimes the gap is temporal: we deliberate in advance of having to act and the deliberation results in a plan for action rather than the action itself. Sometimes there seems to be a gap because, though we have deliberated with a view to action, we do not act on the conclusion and yet the action we perform is both intentional and voluntary. Typical are cases of so-called weakness of will, in which the will seems not to be strong enough to transform the conclusion of the deliberation into action. How then is this gap to be filled?

To fill the gap, we must know what the gap is between. What is the nature of a conclusion of a piece of deliberation or practical reasoning? According to some writers, such as Edgley,[1] the conclusion is an action. According to others[2] the conclusion is that an action is the best thing to do. Another version might argue that the conclusion is that an action is what the agent wants to do. There are further possibilities; the conclusion may be represented as an agent's decision, choice or intention. These various versions are sometimes mistakenly treated as being in competition with each other. Rather different examples of deliberation end in different ways, or can be viewed from different points of view.

Arthur Brown has recently been promoted to the headmastership of a school in which the headmaster has the sole right to use corporal punishment. Gordon Smart has deliberately broken the school rules in a way which, under the previous headmaster, would have automatically led to a caning. Arthur Brown has arranged to see Gordon next day and is trying to make up his mind about what to do. He has taken advice and it overwhelmingly favours a caning. He, himself, is not entirely happy with the rules, and doubts whether breaking the rules in question deserves such a severe punishment. However, he recognises that if his authority is to be respected then he must act by these rules until he can get them changed. He has not previously caned a boy and has a strong dislike of corporal punishment, yet his objections are not so strong as to be a matter of principle. He thinks there are strong arguments for and against caning the boy, but in the end comes to the conclusion that the arguments in favour carry the greatest weight.

He makes a decision about what to do. He is not making a prediction about what he will do, but is forming an intention. Of course such a decision can only be provisional; he has time to revise it. Indeed however near to the point of action an agent is, he can always change his mind. Hence it may be said that no final decision can be made until the agent acts and the action represents the final decision. Even where deliberation takes place some time prior to action and there is no change of mind, the agent may still be said to be reiterating his previous decision, even making it over again. This gives some point to the claim that the conclusion of practical reasoning is an action. Strictly speaking no reasoning is completed except by an action. Moreover thought which is about action, as well as thought which is part of action, can take place without being verbalised,[3] and if it is claimed that the conclusion is an action, a more general account of reasoning and action seems to be possible.

These points are important, and if I were providing a general theory of action, or even of the thinking involved in action, I should have to pay them considerable attention. My concern is more limited, being primarily with those actions which result from deliberation. If an agent deliberates and does not draw his conclusion verbally but merely acts, then he is still doing an action with one feature rather than another. His decision to act in this way rather than any other can be expressed either by specifying the feature verbally, or by doing an action with the feature. I claim, therefore, that an account of deliberation and the explanation of actions which is developed in terms of actions as expressed verbally is not thereby flawed. Indeed my account allows a wider conception of thinking than most of its competitors.

I have already discussed (Chapter IV, Section V) the possibility of re-evaluating one's wants and of forming new wants in such a way that a new conclusion is required. Arthur Brown may think the next morning that he has not given sufficient weight to one factor, or he may be given a new piece of information. If he keeps to the same principles of reasoning as he used before, then taking the new factors into account might indicate a different conclusion.

This is not the only way in which Arthur's action might not conform to his earlier decision. It may be that he is prevented from acting by circumstances outside his control; or it may be that his action shows weakness of will or incontinence. Since I am only concerned with voluntary actions here, I shall deal only with the latter actions. Arthur Brown does not revise his thinking about what he should do, and still recognises that caning the boy is what his reasoning indicates; yet he does not cane the boy. To refrain from caning even in these circumstances may not be judged by some to show the moral inadequacy thought to be typical of examples of weakness of the will. But this is, in fact, an advantage in that the problems of these cases are not confined to ones in which an agent gives in to temptation and acts against his better self. The problem is how an agent can decide that a particular action is the one to do and yet voluntarily do another.

It is not possible to produce one theory to account for all the types of case in which this conflict between reason and action shows itself. Cases of compulsive actions are excluded from consideration. The differences between the other types depend on what kind of conclusion the agent is trying to reach. Arthur Brown, in deliberating, may have been trying to discover, for example, either the morally right action, the objectively prudential action, the action which best serves his own long-term interests, or the action which satisfies his short-term interests. In any of these cases his conclusion might be expressed as a decision about how to act or about what is the best thing to do, there being an unstated assumption about from what point of view it is the best, whether it is from a moral, a prudential, a short-term or a long-term point of view.

According as the aims of the agent's deliberation vary, so will different factors be relevant and vary in the weight they carry and as a result different conclusions will be reached. Arthur Brown may well reach a different conclusion if he is trying to decide, say, what is in his short-term interests from that which he would reach if he was trying to discover what was objectively prudential.

In some cases of weakness of will an agent deliberates towards a conclusion of one type, but acts on what would have been the conclusion of a different type, or what, without reasoning, he thinks such a conclusion would be. An agent reasons about what is the morally right thing to do, but acts in his short-term interests. Many of us like to see ourselves as moral, or at least as rational in the sense of making decisions according to an objective point of view; we find this difficult to live up to, and possibly deceive ourselves about the extent to which we do so. In spite of what we like to think of as our better selves, we act in our short-term interests, or what we feel them to be. Sometimes this is because in deliberation prior to action, we fail to realise how we will feel when the situation in which action is required occurs. An example may make this clearer.

Peter Paine is due for a check-up at the dentist and is sure that treatment will be required. He realises the pain he is likely to suffer on this visit is much less than the long-term pain he would get from not having his teeth treated. However when it comes to going to the dentist his reaction to the thought of imminent pain is of quite a different order from the reaction he predicted and took account of in deliberating. The result is an impulse-desire against going to the dentist which may be so strong that he changes his mind. When reflecting afterwards on his failure to do the sensible or rational thing, the situation becomes more like that in which he made his original decision than that he was faced with when called on to act. Hence he may feel guilt and even puzzlement at his own failure. When looked at objectively, and not from inside the situation in which he had to act, his action is clearly against his interests. But one's immediate interests, because related to the situation one is in, are more strongly felt than their intrinsic nature deserves.

Deliberation requires not only a capacity for reasoning and judgment but also imagination. In deciding what to do in a future situation, I have to take account of what my wants are likely to be in that situation. This requires imagination, not only about my reaction to possible pain and pleasure, but also to other emotions. Sometimes an agent's imagination is not adequate, and when he comes to act an impulse-desire which is so much stronger than was anticipated takes him by surprise, and overcomes the strength of other feature-wants by its very unexpectedness. It is not that the impulse-desire is so strong that it could not have been controlled; it is rather that, perhaps in spite of himself, the agent lets the impulse-desire overcome what he coolly and dispassionately took to be his feature-wants. He may not always disapprove of such impulse-desires. Arthur Brown may find that when actually in the situation of having to cane Gordon, he finds that inflicting physical pain is abhorrent to him; it is this which prevents him from doing what he rationally thought would be best. Though his feelings are a surprise to him, he may nevertheless welcome them and think they ought to carry weight. Sometimes the calculated action is wrong, while the spontaneous action which expresses an immediately aroused, deeply felt and perhaps unsuspected emotion can be right.

I have not emphasised sufficiently that if deliberation is to lead to action then at some point the agent must be motivated, and hence either the conclusion includes a motivational element or else there is a gap between accepting the conclusion and acting on it. To reach a conclusion about what it is sensible, rational or best to do may seem to indicate practical deliberation has taken place, but, depending on the context, it may not motivate. It is a conclusion analogous to what an agent likes or wishes were so, rather than to one about what an agent wants.

Is it, in fact, possible to deliberate and reach a conclusion about what is wanted? On some accounts of wants that would only be possible if wants were built into the premises. However, I have argued that an agent can form his own wants, and can evaluate his wants, whether impulse-desires or feature-wants of his own making. If this is so, then an agent must be able to motivate himself. There are limits to how successfully an agent can do so. The stronger and the less anticipated an impulse-desire is, the more difficult is it for an agent to resist it. An impulse-desire because of its strength can carry more weight than the agent would wish. Often we would like to do the rational or sensible action, but without considerable effort, and sometimes in spite of considerable effort, we are unable to do it. We cannot motivate ourselves in such a way as to act in opposition to such impulse-desires. It follows from this that a picture of the agent—who is not subject to compulsive desires—as essentially rational and as assessing and evaluating his feature-wants as he thinks fit can need correction.

Impulse-desires vary in strength: at one end of the scale they exert little motivational force, and the extent to which they are satisfied depends on the agent's evaluation; at the other end they are compulsive and cannot be resisted; in between the stronger they are the more the agent is motivated to satisfy them independently of his evaluation of them. But what is the relation between the strength of an impulse-desire and the weight an agent gives to it? Suppose an agent has a very strong thirst: he may recognise its strength and yet give it a negative evaluation. He acknowledges its strong motivational force, and that it will take much resistance. Whether he is able to resist it depends on his evaluation of it and on his other feature-wants. His judgment of the impulse-desire will attempt to alter the motivational force it has and whether or not he is motivated by the impulse-desire depends on the extent to which that judgment and other feature-wants—as judged by him—motivate him. In some cases in which the impulse-desires could be controlled, the agent fails to reduce sufficiently the motivational force of the impulse-desire, or fails to find or give sufficient force to his other feature-wants; the conclusion of his deliberation reflects his judgments rather than the strength of the impulse-desire, and so his action is not that suggested by his deliberation but rather satisfies the impulse-desire. It displays weakness of will.

I have given an account of various ways in which cases of weakness of will can be explained.[4] This account is not, and could not be, either systematic or comprehensive. No one simple theory can account for all instances. Nevertheless the accounts of practical reasoning and of wants which I have given seem to me to provide the tools with which to explain most, if not all, instances.

Let me return now to ordinary actions and sum up my view about the link between deliberation and action. An agent deliberates and reaches a conclusion; that conclusion may be of various sorts, depending on the aim of the agent in deliberating. Deciding on the objectively best action is different from deciding what one wants to do, in that the former carries less motivational weight than the latter. If the deliberation is of the latter type, then, in the absence of any revision, it will be acted on. But at any point until he acts an agent can revise his conclusion. In so far as he sticks to it he has not used the opportunity he has of making a revision: he allows his decision to take its course, but he does not need to do so. To say that an action is voluntary is to say that the agent could have acted differently. In order to have acted differently he would have had to give different weight to his reasons—or even to have had different reasons. This implies that he would have had to evaluate the relevant factors in a different way. Thus the voluntariness of an action is equivalent to the agent having been able to evaluate differently or to re-evaluate. An agent must, then, have the ability to re-evaluate up to the point of action. If he does not do so he is re-affirming the decision he reached in his deliberation, and re-affirming his commitment to the evaluations he made in it.

VIII
Explaining by Reasons

I—Reasons and feature-wants

My discussion of the way actions originate has prepared the ground for an account of the way reasons explain an action, since to explain it is to show why it was performed, what led to it or produced it. If the action is deliberative then to understand how it came about is to understand the process of deliberation which ends with the agent doing it. It may be said that understanding how an action came about and explaining an action are not the same. Perhaps not, but they are certainly closely related. Insofar as there is a difference the former might be a narrative of the events, both physical and psychological, which led up to the action; while the latter must pick out events, states of affairs or conditions without which the action would not have occurred. Any explanation of an action must mention one or more factors which explain why the action happened. These factors cannot be wholly outside the deliberative process if it is as a result of this deliberation that the agent does the action. From the narrative of the deliberation we clearly leave out any part which is incidental, which has nothing to do with the conclusion being reached, and pick out those parts which are most important to the particular conclusion being reached, those parts of the deliberation which are essential for it to have ended in the way it did. From the account of deliberation given what is picked out must be those of his feature-wants the agent thinks most important. What leads to his conclusion about what to do is his evaluation of certain feature-wants as being decisively important in this situation.

Consider, again, the case of Thomas Fagg (Chapter II, Section II). Let us suppose that in his deliberation about whether to give up smoking he decides in the end to give it up because of its effect on his health. His reason is given as that effect or, more fully, as his belief that smoking would damage his health and his desire to avoid such damage. To say this is to say that the possible damage to his health is the feature he thinks most important. It outweighs in his evaluation all other features associated with continuing to smoke; moreover it is the effect on his health, rather than any other features of giving up smoking, which outweighs those features which would have led to a conclusion against giving up.

We do not always state a reason fully. Sometimes what is mentioned is a fact, a desire, some other kind of feeling or emotion, or a belief. Why did you not take the short-cut? It was too steep; I wanted to take more than an hour to get here; I was afraid of having an accident; I thought the longer route was safer. All of these are acceptable replies, and all perfectly consistent with each other. In each case what is stated as the reason can be filled out by giving a belief and a feature-want. In actual explanations there is rarely any need to do so, because the belief and the feature-want will be obvious from whatever feature is mentioned.

The reason for an action relates to the feature-want, or to the feature the agent took to be most important. However, this needs qualification, since in giving an actual explanation it is not always that particular reason which is given. In fact, it is possible to have several different explanations for the same action, the difference depending on the grounds of one's interest in finding an explanation. They largely arise from the fact that the same action may be described in different ways, and thus the demand for an explanation can take different forms. 'Why did you not take the short-cut?', may get a different answer from 'Why did you take the long way round?', or from 'Why did you go past the Post Office?' In answering the first question the reasons against the route not taken are likely to be mentioned; while with the second it is more likely to be reasons in favour of the route taken; and with the third any reasons there were for going past the Post Office. If the reasons are simple, and one reason dominates all the others, then no doubt that reason is the one to be given, whatever form the request for an explanation takes. But where the reasons are complex, where the agent has a number of feature-wants in favour of the action he takes, then it is not always the most important reason which is mentioned: he may have arrived at his decision because of a number of feature-wants which favour his action and a number which are against the actions he did not take. Any one of these may be picked out, depending on why an explanation is required or why the action is puzzling. In explaining an action we thus abstract from the process by which the action is arrived at. It is rarely important to mention many of the agent's feature-wants, or the way he deliberated about them. But in giving an account of the relation of the agent's reason to the action it explains, it is important to remember that the reason has been abstracted from his deliberation as a whole, just as it is important to remember that the deliberation is abstracted from the wider context of assumptions, beliefs, emotions, values and much else which may be neither explicit nor understood.

II—*Reasons are evaluations*

According to the usual account of reasons, the reason which explains an action produces that action, and since a reason consists of a feature-want and a belief it would seem to follow that the feature-want and the belief produce and—if a causal view is taken—cause the action. I dispute this. It is the case that without the feature-want and the belief which form the reason for his action the agent would not have done the action. But his having them is not sufficient for the action to follow; whether or not it does, depends on his evaluation of the feature-want. It is possible to construct cases where two agents have the same beliefs and feature-wants, and yet the one acts to satisfy the feature-want and the other does not. The difference between them lies in the different ways they evaluate that feature-want. To say that a belief and a feature-want constitute one of the agent's reasons—let alone his only reason—is to say more than that he has them; it is to say that he has decided that they are to be a reason or the reason for his doing the action. It is his decision which turns them into a reason. In explaining an action by saying that a factor is the reason for it, we are not merely mentioning the presence of that factor or its connection with the action; we are also saying something about the way it is connected through the agent's evaluation of it.

Rachel is pregnant and discovers that there is a more than fifty-fifty chance that the baby will be born disabled. After some thought she decides to have an abortion, her reason being that she wants any child of hers to have the chance of a full life. To say that this is her reason is not only to say that she has that want, but also that she evaluates that want highly, or more highly than other wants relevant to the situation. To show more clearly what this involves, I shall consider Davidson's account of reasons and the way the reason explains the action.[1] He calls such explanations rationalisations. He begins by outlining informally what he means by a primary reason. It consists of a 'pro attitude toward actions of a certain kind' and a belief 'that his action is of that kind'.[2] Before going on to examine the relation between a primary reason and the related action it is necessary to look more closely at what Davidson means by a pro-attitude. Under pro-attitude, he says, are to be included:

desires, wantings, urges, promptings, and a great variety of moral views, aesthetic principles, economic prejudices, social conventions, and public and private goals and values in so far as these can be interpreted as attitudes of an agent directed toward actions of a certain kind. The word 'attitude' does yeoman service here, for it must cover not only permanent character traits that show themselves in a lifetime of behaviour, like love of children or a taste for loud company, but also the most passing fancy that prompts a unique action, like a sudden desire to touch a woman's elbow.[3]

In saying this he is making clear a use which is different from mine. I differentiate between pro-attitudes and feature-wants; in my usage the former are favourable attitudes, such as approving or liking, but without any element of action-guiding; the latter are pro-attitudes to which an action-guiding or motivating component is added. The distinction I make is important and is at the heart of the logical connection argument as developed by Melden.[4] It is not clear whether Davidson thinks there is no distinction here, or whether he intends pro-attitudes to be restricted to action-guiding attitudes. Most of the examples he mentions can be interpreted as action-guiding, and I shall take his pro-attitudes to be equivalent to what I have called feature-wants.

Davidson makes his claim about the way reasons rationalise by formulating

C_1. R is a primary reason why an agent performed the action A under the description d only if R consists of a pro attitude of the agent toward actions with a certain property, and a belief of the agent that A, under the description d, has that property.[5]

He adds a second condition which the agent's primary reason for his action must fulfil:

In order to turn the first 'and' to 'because' in 'He exercised *and* he wanted to reduce and thought exercise would do it', we must, as the basic move, augment condition C_1 with:
C_2. A primary reason for an action is its cause.[6]

I accept that C_1 is a necessary condition for any reason to fulfil if a pro-attitude is taken to be a feature-want. I further accept that C_1 is not sufficient by itself: an agent may well have a feature-want and a belief which could constitute his reason for his action, but which nevertheless do not do so. Davidson is right in thinking that we need a further condition in order to turn the first 'and' to 'because'. However I shall argue that C_2 is not the required condition. In order to state the argument clearly I shall use the notion of a *prima facie* reason for whatever fulfils C_1, whether or not it fulfils C_2 or any replacement for C_2. Thus the second condition may be said to be designed to distinguish between a *prima facie* reason which is in fact the agent's reason for his action, and the rest of his *prima facie* reasons, no one of which is his reason.

Before looking at Davidson's example in detail it is worth stating what I take to be two main points of difficulty with his argument. The first is that the distinction between the case in which the *prima facie* reason is the agent's reason and the case in which it is not is made no clearer by saying that in the one case the *prima facie* reason is a cause and in the other it is not. What is needed for Davidson's view to be acceptable is an account of how a *prima facie* reason becomes a cause, what it is that turns it into a cause, or what criteria we need to decide whether a *prima facie* reason is a cause. Without such an account the claim that the primary reason is a cause tells us little, and says nothing about what an agent's reason is and how it relates to his action.

The second point is that Davidson's argument leads to difficulties in distinguishing between the explanations of voluntary actions and the explanations of compulsive actions. In fact Davidson's characterisation of a reason would serve well as the characterisation of an internal cause of a compulsive action. The alcoholic's desire for alcohol can be filled out as a *prima facie* reason, and such a desire would in some cases be the cause of his action. To be fair to Davidson he says in a footnote that his two conditions are only necessary, but that he believes C_2 can be strengthened to make the conditions sufficient as well. I am not sure whether in making such an admission he had in mind the point I am making. Its relegation to a footnote makes it doubtful whether Davidson was thinking of anything so crucial. However, my argument is that Davidson's conditions are neither necessary nor sufficient in any obvious sense of 'cause'. I shall try to show that what I have said about the processes of deliberation makes it possible to sort out the difficulties which lead Davidson to formulate C_2, and also allows a distinction between the origination of deliberative actions by reasons and of those involuntary but intentional actions which arise from internal or mental causes.

Let us look at Davidson's example. It can be set out in terms of the following three statements:

(1) He exercised.
(2) He wanted to reduce and thought exercise would do it.
(3) He exercised because he wanted to reduce.

We can then make a contrast between two agents, Michael Fitt and Dominic Joy, both of whom have exercised and both of whom want to reduce. (1) and (2) are true of both of them. The contrast lies in the fact that while (3) is true of Michael it is not true of Dominic. I shall assume in discussing this example that they have both deliberated and are aware of the truth or falsehood of these statements. Thus in the process of their deliberation it has occurred to both of them that they want to reduce and that exercise will do it. In both cases we can suppose the conditions for a *prima facie* reason are satisfied. According to Davidson, if Michael Fitt's reason for exercising is given by (3), then condition C_2 must be satisfied and (3) must state a causal link between the *prima facie* reason and the action. For Dominic Joy the conditions for a *prima facie* reason are also satisfied but C_2 is not, and thus this *prima facie* reason is not his reason for exercising.

The contrast between these two cases can be analysed in more detail. Take first, Dominic Joy. He recognises the truth of (2) but thinks it irrelevant—or, perhaps more likely, unimportant—in making up his mind about whether or not to exercise. The fact that he wants to reduce is not something to which he attaches much weight in making his decision. He has the feature-want, but his evaluation of that feature-want is not high. If the consideration which in fact leads him to exercise—his enjoyment of it—had not been present, his wanting to reduce would not have been sufficient to outweigh the feature-wants which were against his exercising. For Michael Fitt, on the other hand, it is the truth of (2) which leads him to decide in favour of exercising. Thus the difference between Michael and Dominic is that Michael, unlike Dominic, thinks his desire to reduce sufficiently important and other factors so much less important that the desire is decisive. Michael puts a high value on this feature-want relative to his other feature-wants, while Dominic puts a low value on it. There are, of course, difficulties about verifying the various claims of the two agents about their decisions and the grounds on which they make them, but I shall not discuss these here as they do not affect the distinction being made (see Chapter XIII).

It may seem that the contrast this example illustrates is always clear-cut; the difference between the two cases lies simply in the attitudes of each man towards wanting to reduce, the one thinking it decisive and the other thinking it irrelevant. This might seem to imply that these were the only two possible attitudes an agent could have towards a feature-want. Clearly this is not so. Eileen Bird, who is in similar circumstances to Michael and Dominic, gives a different emphasis to wanting to reduce. For her it is one of a variety of reasons why she exercises. She takes this feature-want into account in making the decision, so that it has some effect on the action but is not in itself decisive. Eileen's evaluation of it is not such as to make it alone sufficient to outweigh those of her feature-wants which point in a different direction. Equally those of her other feature-wants which favoured exercising might not in themselves be sufficiently highly valued to lead her to exercise without having wanted to reduce. An agent can have a variety of different attitudes towards her *prima facie* reasons and give different evaluations to them. But whether she thinks that a *prima facie* reason is irrelevant, decisive, or something between the two, is for her to decide. It is so not because she is the only person with the required knowledge of herself, but because without her decision the *prima facie* reason cannot become either her only reason or one among several. In order to make up her mind about what to do she must evaluate her *prima facie* reasons. It is this evaluation which turns the *prima facie* reason into her reason. This point may seem to be perfectly compatible with Davidson's suggestions that to be the agent's reason a primary reason must be the cause of the action. I shall argue in Chapter X that to put the relation between reason and action in this way is misleading.

I have tried to solve—for deliberative actions at least—the problem of what turns a *prima facie* reason into the agent's reason in terms of his attitude towards or his evaluation of it. This may suggest that the agent must know and is the only person who can know which of his *prima facie* reasons is the reason for his action. However, it may be pointed out that, even where an agent has deliberated, he may be unsure about which *prima facie* reason is his reason and whether it is his only reason. In some cases he may indeed be wrong about his reasons. It is easy to imagine a case where an agent is jealous of someone; he knows he is jealous, knows that his feelings of jealousy may affect what he does, acts in the way he would have acted if he had been so affected, and yet sincerely claims that such feelings do not affect his action, though an observer

Explaining by Reasons

may be sure that he is mistaken and that they do.

There are various ways in which the agent may be mistaken about why he is doing an action. On the whole people want their actions to be explicable in terms of reasons, and reasons which are not discreditable. When an agent is giving an explanation of a past action the giving of the explanation is itself an action: he has feature-wants which may not be satisfied if the correct explanation is given. How far those feature-wants operate as reasons and how far as causes over which the agent has no control may vary from case to case. For example, someone who refuses a cigarette after being told to do so under hypnosis may provide a rationalisation of his refusal which does not mention the hypnosis. He is clearly mistaken: he did not act from a reason, but rather his action was caused. He rationalises his action either because he wants there to be a reason, or because he assumes there is a reason; but perhaps, above all, because he does not know about the causative factor. There are problems about unconscious reasons and about self-deception (Chapter XI, Section IV), but there is nothing I have said about reasons and the agent's evaluation of feature-wants to suggest the impossibility of his being mistaken about what he has done or what has happened to him.

I pointed out earlier that Davidson's account failed to provide a way of distinguishing between a compulsive action caused by feature-wants and an action freely chosen on the basis of the same feature-want. That is a distinction which my account allows. The agent may be mistaken about the relation of his feature-wants or his *prima facie* reasons to his action. An agent may have a feature-want or a relevant *prima facie* reason consisting of a pro-attitude and a belief; his attitude to it or his evaluation of it may be irrelevant and, however he evaluates it, the action which satisfies the feature-want results. In this case the *prima facie* reason is the cause of his action but is not his *reason* for it. On the other hand, in the case where that evaluation is essential to the action, the *prima facie* reason is not the cause in the same sense. It may be claimed that in the latter case the evaluation turns the *prima facie* reason into the cause, but a cause of a different kind from that in the former case. Again I shall point out in Chapter X the difficulties of having two kinds of cause, and of a reason being a cause of any kind. In the meantime I suggest that my account allows the required distinction to be made.

My argument has been that what turns the 'and' into a 'because' in Davidson's example is the agent's evaluation of—and decision about—his wanting to reduce. This evaluation has to be taken in the context of the other factors relevant to his decision about what to do. His evaluation when his wanting to reduce is his reason for exercising is different from the one he makes when it is not his reason but another *prima facie* reason is. Within the account of reasons I have given it is possible to make this distinction, and Davidson is mistaken in thinking it necessary to introduce the notion of cause.

III—*Reasons and rules*

Reasons are thought by Kant and others to necessarily involve a reference to a rule or principle, and this view seems to be connected with the claim that deliberation can only involve deduction. It is therefore worth considering not only in order to show that it is wrong, but also to clarify further the account of reasons I am giving.

Kant's view, at least according to his interpreters, is that motivation which is not impulsive must involve a maxim or principle: 'An action done from duty has its moral worth, *not in the purpose* to be attained by it, but in the maxim in accordance with which it is decided upon.'[7] As Paton suggests:

> ... Kant is trying to mark a real difference between human conduct and animal behaviour. In acting, a human being does not, unless in very exceptional circumstances, respond blindly to impulse. He knows what he is doing; he recognises the quality of his action; and he could not do this without some concept, however vague, of the principle on which he acts.[8]

Kant gives his view in the context of a discussion of morality, and that is where this assumption is most often found. For instance, Hare suggests:

There are two factors which may be involved in the making of any decision to do something . . . They correspond to the major and minor premisses of the Aristotelian practical syllogism. The major premiss is a principle of conduct; the minor premiss is a statement, more or less full, of what we should in fact be doing if we did one or other of the alternatives open to us.[9]

He elaborates his views in relation to an artificial example: he considers a man who has no principles of conduct, has full knowledge of the consequences of different courses open to him and chooses one course. If asked why he chose it, he might answer in one of two ways. 'He might say "I can't give any reasons" . . . On the other hand, he might say "It was this and this that made me decide".'[10] If he gives the second answer he has started to form principles for himself: 'for to choose effects *because* they are such and such is to begin to act on a principle that such and such effects are to be chosen'.[11] Thus to choose for a reason is to have a principle and to base one's choice on one's principle. This is a more explicit statement of the view which I take Kant to assume.[12]

In arguing against such an account as this care must be taken to avoid arguing only against a particular view about the nature of rules. It may be easy to show the difficulties in a ten-commandment view of rules, or in the view that there is one and only one principle of morality, which when applied to particular circumstances gives the correct moral judgment for that situation. What the argument is really about is whether acting on a reason necessarily involves the idea of a rule or principle, or whether there is any concept of a rule according to which acting for a reason means acting on the related rule.

Consider the following characterisation of a rule which is adapted from Mabbott.[13] To say that an action falls under a rule is to say that the action is a member of a class of acts which have some common character. Such a rule will then say either that all actions having such a character are to be done, or that such actions are to be generally done, or that actions having such a character are to be done if certain conditions are satisfied. If this is accepted, then it follows that the thesis under discussion is that acting for a reason implies acting because the action is a member of a class of acts which have some common characteristic: it is further implied that it is accepted that all actions with this characteristic are to be done—or at least are *prima facie* to be done.

Clearly if I do an action for a reason I do that action because of a characteristic the action has, a characteristic determined by the reason. It will then be the same to say of an action that it falls under a rule as to say that it is done for a reason. Both the rule and the reason mention a characteristic because of which the action is performed. However, the second part of the definition of a rule gives more trouble. It seems to me possible to do an action for a reason and yet not to accept the rule, not to be acting on the rule, and not to have the rule as the basis for one's action.

Let us go back to Hare's example of the man who has no principles of conduct, and says that he is doing the action because it has certain effects and that it is these which make him decide to act in such a way. I do not see in what useful sense it can be said that he must have started to form principles for himself. Of course he may have done so: he may have decided not only that at that time and in that particular situation certain effects would lead him to decide on this action, but also that the same effects in other situations should lead him to decide on the same kind of action, or at least should influence him or be relevant to his decision. But does he need to do so? Let us take an example. Suppose Joseph Appleby is asked why he is playing his trumpet. His response is that he is playing it because the noise will annoy his next-door neighbour, Mrs. Grump. (The same example is used for a somewhat different purpose in Chapter III, Section IV.) His action thus falls under the rule: Actions which annoy Mrs. Grump are usually to be performed. I am not sure whether this would be the rule Hare would suggest or whether it would have to be universal, leaving out any reference to an individual.[14] Even then it would have a low-degree of generality in that it would only apply to a restricted number of situations. If the rule has to be universal or if it has to be more rather than less general, then it is less likely that Joseph Appleby accepts it. Therefore I shall consider the relation of his action to the rule I have given.

Joseph Appleby's action comes under the rule of annoying Mrs. Grump: the rule and his reason mention the same characteristic. In one sense he would not have done it if it had not come under the rule, for if the action has not come under the rule it would not have had the characteristic of annoying Mrs. Grump. A further claim might be made—he did the action *because* it came under the rule. But does it follow that he must accept the rule? I do not think so. It is the ambiguity of the 'because' in that claim which gives rise to difficulties. The claim could mean that the action is of the sort which falls under the rule, and because it is of that sort it is done. Or it could mean that the action is done because the rule is accepted. This would be quite a different claim. It would suggest that in acting on a reason an agent implicitly accepts that the reason would also be at least relevant in other similar circumstances. This suggestion needs careful examination.

To say that an action one has done or has decided to do is a member of a class defined by a characteristic goes no further than saying that the action has that characteristic. To say that an action is done for a reason is to say that the action has that characteristic, and that the agent has made the required evaluation of the feature-want which is directed towards the characteristic. Does this imply anything about whether one would do other actions with that characteristic? Joseph Appleby's playing of his trumpet has the characteristic of annoying Mrs. Grump. He wants to annoy her, and he gives more weight to or evaluates more highly this feature-want than others. Do these facts commit him to any view about other actions at other times aimed at annoying Mrs. Grump or any other next door neighbour? I can see no logical inconsistency in his saying that on this occasion he is acting to annoy Mrs. Grump, and that annoying her may not at other times be a reason for him to act in this way. There are arguments against this. For instance it might be alleged that it is only because the reasons are not fully stated that there appears to be no commitment to other actions of the same kind. If the reasons were stated in terms of wanting to annoy

Mrs. Grump under these specific circumstances might there then not be a commitment? Does not the nature of wants imply there must be? Wanting X gives one a reason, though not necessarily a sufficient reason, for doing whatever will achieve X. I agree that this follows from what was said about feature-wants, but we cannot extract any rule from the connection between wants and reasons except that whenever he wants to annoy his next-door neighbour he will have a reason for doing so. His now wanting to annoy her does not even imply that this want will continue, and that he will have it whenever the circumstances repeat themselves, whether as an impulse-desire or as a deliberative feature-want. Nor does the fact that this want now constitutes a sufficient reason mean that whenever he has the want it will constitute a sufficient reason.

This, it may be said, misses the point of Hare's reference to rules or principles. To try and discover that point, let us look at the way a reason is expanded so as to mention further relevant characteristics of the present situation. Certainly Joseph Appleby's reason is a simplification of the grounds of his action. My account of reasons implies that. Some further conditions need to be satisfied, and some others must fail to be satisfied, before his stated reason will be a sufficient reason. Suppose a full statement of his reasons and the relevant conditions is given. Would it not then be the case that whenever all of these were satisfied he would have sufficient reason for doing the same action? Maybe Joseph Appleby had just been annoyed by the noise of the television next-door; maybe he also needs to practise his trumpet, or at least is not fed up with playing it. If these circumstances repeat themselves, would he not then have a reason, even a sufficient reason, for playing his trumpet? If he does not play it, would he not be inconsistent? To act differently under the same circumstances, it is suggested, is either to be inconsistent or to change one's evaluations. If an agent acts differently in two similar situations there must be a reason for his doing so. He must be able to point either to differences in the external situation or in his attitude towards that situation. Thus the agent must accept a rule determined by his reasons, a rule which merely states that whenever the circumstances are the same he should act in the same way.

It is difficult to know how far it is possible to disagree with this argument. In one form it seems to be saying that if one acts on a reason, then if circumstances are the same and one has not changed one's mind one would act on that reason again. Not to do so is by definition to have changed one's mind. I have no reluctance about accepting this, so long as it is not taken to imply that one cannot or should not change one's mind, or to imply that in acting on a reason there is a commitment not to change one's mind. However, this is not the position which Kant and Hare seem to be assuming. For them there is a rule implicit in a reason, and that rule has some significance. Both mention fairly specific rules, with little or nothing in the way of qualifying conditions. Joseph Appleby may agree that if he is not of a different mind and the circumstances are the same he will act so as to annoy Mrs. Grump. But to agree to this does not commit him—as Kant and Hare would seem to suggest—to a principle of always annoying her, or even to that principle when qualified by a list of exceptions or conditions which have to be satisfied for the principle to apply, a list which must be limited and fully stated for the principle to work as a rule.

When an agent acts for a particular reason, the feature mentioned in the reason must be sufficient to lead the agent to decide on the action, and other features must be explicitly or implicitly dismissed as less important. From this we can tell little about the agent's reactions to other actions with this feature: we cannot tell that the rest of the features—whether the same or different from those of the original action—will be dismissed as unimportant. The fact that on one occasion he thought the presence of the factor sufficient to constitute a reason for acting may be an indication that the factor is of some importance to him, and therefore one might infer that he would take it into account on other occasions. However, he may not do so and yet in no way have changed his values or been inconsistent. What is important in one context may be unimportant in another. To return what one has borrowed from a neighbour may be important in normal circumstances, but becomes totally unimportant in the context of a great calamity. The fact that the sun is shining may be a sufficient reason for taking a walk on one occasion, and may be irrelevant on many other occasions, without there being any inconsistency. Moreover, it is in principle impossible to specify the occasions on which a factor may or may not be relevant or sufficient. The future is not wholly predictable and all situations are different, even if only in minor respects. Thus though a factor may have been a reason on a previous occasion, a new decision will still be needed about it when it is part of a new situation. This is not to deny that some situations may be so similar that fresh thought does not need to be given to the factor; nevertheless there is an implicit decision about the situation being similar and about the factor in relation to it.

My suggestion about reasons is that they need not indicate a rule in any usual sense of the term. To say that I do this action because of a characteristic X does not imply that any action with characteristic X should be done, or even that all such actions should *prima facie* be done. It is true that there is often an element of generality in reasons, though there need not be. Most people tend to go on thinking the same things important: our feature-wants have a certain degree of stability. We may therefore make certain generalisations about the kind of features which tend to give us a reason for action. Such generalisations may be made about one person, about some people or about all people. We may argue that such generalisations ought to hold, and that the presence of a certain feature constitutes a reason not just for one agent but for all people. We may argue that in certain cases anyone who does not agree that the feature provides a reason is mistaken or misguided. There are, it may be said, certain norms about what should influence actions. But these norms do not need to be stated as rules, even though they sometimes are. I would argue that in most cases they are better stated in terms of reasons, in terms of a factor being a good reason for acting. It may be that one feature is taken to be so important as very often, if not always, to override all other considerations, and in this case a rule may usefully be given and adherence to it advocated on moral or prudential grounds. However, it is only rarely that this can be done. There may be some people who try to guide their lives by reference to rules, though it is difficult to see how they can do so, and how they can sort out in advance cases of conflict, or decide on the way the rules are to apply. But my argument is not about whether it is possible for someone to determine their actions by reference to rules or whether it is right or wrong to do so, though it may indicate my views about these matters: my argument is that reasons do not necessarily imply rules and that, while the pattern of deliberation appropriate to rules may be deductive, this will not work for reasons in general.

If reasons must involve rules, then deduction seems the appropriate form for practical reasoning, and vice versa. To reject rules, as the existentialist does, implies either an alternative pattern of thinking, or that actions are not rational, but rather a matter of caprice. For an existentialist like Sartre[15] situations are unique, and he might sometimes be thought to be suggesting that there is nothing to be said about the way in which choices are to be made and that there are no reasons for choosing one way rather than another. But for him such choices are not a matter of caprice, because of the consequences and the element of self-commitment and self-determination involved in the decision; this is so even though we cannot lay down rules about how to make these choices and there is no standard procedure by which the right answers about what to do may be reached. Sartre is right, but this does not imply that we cannot reason and deliberate about what to do. To deny the necessity or the possibility of rules does not imply that reasoning is impossible. We can admit the criticisms of accounts of reasoning in terms of rules which I have made, and which are implicit in an existentialist view of morality, and yet accept the possibility and the advisability of reasoning, whether in determining action in general or only moral action. The view of deliberation I have developed allows for this. We can go through a detailed process of considering how various factors affect different courses of action and in the light of this evaluate them. This does not involve a reference to rules, and can be done while paying due attention to the particularity of the situation. How far we bring different but comparable situations into our deliberation is a matter for discussion. Certainly we cannot isolate the present situation from what has happened and what may happen. The values we hold and the ways we judge are likely to have, indeed should have, a certain constancy about them; but that constancy does not need to be enshrined in a set of rules.

My conclusion is that acting for a reason does not require that the agent should be acting on a rule. An account can be given of reasons and deliberation which does not depend on rules. Further it is not possible to give an adequate and complete account of decision-making in terms of rules and a deductive account of reasoning which is usually associated with a reliance on rules.

This completes my account of reasons as they explain deliberative actions. Its essential features are:

(i) A *prima facie* reason consists of a feature-want together with a belief that the action being explained satisfies the feature-want.

(ii) The reasons why an agent does an action are those of his *prima facie* reasons which are satisfied by the action, and which the agent has evaluated as being worth satisfying or as more worth satisfying than other *prima facie* reasons.

IX
Reasons and the Logical Connection Argument

I—Melden's version of the argument
The logical connection argument claims that reasons are logically connected with the actions they explain and, since causes and their effects must be logically independent, reasons cannot be causes. There is no difficulty in finding criticisms of this argument?[1] Indeed, in my view, both premises—when interpreted in the most obvious way—are false and cannot support the conclusion. Nevertheless the argument indicates something important about the way reasons explain. I shall try to show what this is and how it prevents causal views taking a form which has the implications which I think Melden and others have rightly wanted to reject.

To suppose, Melden argues, that the motive for an action is a cause of it is self-contradictory:

> As the alleged cause of the action, it cannot serve further to characterize the action. As motive it must—for it tells us what in fact the person was doing. It informs us, *qua* motive, that the action of raising the arm was in fact the action of giving information to others to the effect that the driver was preparing to make a turn. Now this . . . is in effect to make it clear that the action of raising the arm was indeed the action of signalling. In short, citing the motive was giving a fuller characterization of the action; it was indeed providing a better understanding of what the driver was doing.[2]

The claim is that a cause and its effect must be distinct and logically independent, while motives need not be. In the case of many actions for which there is a motive there is no prior mental event—there is nothing other than the action itself. The motive must be part of the action rather than anything antecedent to the action. To give the motive, it is suggested, is to say what the agent's intention is in acting. Rather than being about an intention which had been previously formed, it is about the action itself and gives a description of the action. The intention cannot be separated from the action, and to describe the one is to describe the other. Thus the intention is logically connected with the action and in the same way so are the motive and the reason; hence explanations by reasons must belong to a different type from causal explanations. Melden uses the same kind of argument in relation to desires and wants:

> The supposition, then, that desiring or wanting is a Humean cause, some sort of internal tension or uneasiness, involves the following contradiction: As Humean cause or internal impression, it must be describable without reference to anything else—object desired, the action of getting or the action of trying to get the thing desired; but as desire this is impossible.[3]

The grounds for alleging that wants, desires, motives and reasons are logically connected with the related actions is that they cannot be characterised without reference to their objects, and that to desire or want something, to have a motive or reason for something, entails trying to get what is wanted or trying to do the action for which one has the motive or reason.

There are several subsidiary strands in Melden's argument. One is that to explain by reasons or desires is 'to explain not how these actions . . . are produced, but rather how these same actions . . . can be more fully understood as the actions they are in fact'.[4] He is distinguishing between two types of explanation, the one concerned with how things came about and the other with what things are; he claims that explanations by reasons belong to the latter type. Another strand is the claim that desires, wants, motives and reasons cannot be internal events, that 'no internal impression could possibly exhibit the logical features of a desire'.[5] A third strand is that causes and their effects must be logically independent, and so any things which are logically connected cannot be causally related. There is much else in his argument which I shall not deal with and even the third strand is only very briefly discussed.

II—What- and why- explanations

Consider Melden's notion of explanation.[6] He argues that in explaining an action one is making clear what it is one is doing, making sense of what is puzzling, or that one 'reveals an order or pattern in the proceedings which had not been apparent'.[7] Let me apply this to an example. Suppose someone is puzzled about what I am doing. I may explain it by saying that I am mending a fuse. But that much may already be clear to him; what he wants to know is exactly what I am doing in mending it. He wants to have the various steps explained to him, perhaps so that he can learn how to do it for himself. The explanation may then give a more detailed description and analysis of the action.

Again suppose one is given a message which at first sight seems a mere jumble of words which mean nothing. One cannot see what is being said or what the point of the message is. To explain it is to show that there is order rather than chaos and what that order is; an attempt is made to convey in other words what the message is—it is restated. Again the particular significance of puzzling words may be shown. The explanation is not concerned with the origin of the message or what led to its being sent, for that is the explanation of something different, even though it may help to explain what the message is. Thus we get a contrast between two types of explanation, why-explanations and what-explanations. The former explain why something has occurred or why it is as it is, and thus give an account of the origination of that which is being explained. The most straight-forward are causal explanations of physical happenings. Why does lightning occur? Why did this fuse blow? In the case of the message the why-explanation tells us why the message was sent or what led to its being sent.

In contrast there are what-explanations, which explain what something is, what the message consists of. It may be a line of a poem or a painting, a motor-car or a hieroglyph. We can even explain events in this way. What is happening when the car moves? What is happening when the lightning flashes? We can explain ceremonial events or traditional customs, not by saying what led people to participate in them or what their origins are, but by explaining what is happening in them, what various people are doing or what is their meaning. Such explanations are not of how things come about: they do not try to show the action or event, poem or machine as part of a process, nor do they show it to be the result of antecedent events, though it may be necessary to do this in order to understand what they are.

Part of Melden's argument can be expressed by saying that causal explanations are why-explanations and explanations by reasons are what-explanations. Such what-explanations consist of redescribing the object of the explanation; they do not link two distinct or independent actions but rather mention only the action being explained for which an alternative description is found. Rebecca's action in standing up is explained in terms of her intention of getting a better view. To state her intention is to redescribe — even to describe more accurately — her action. Her having that intention is not a separate event from her action, and therefore to explain in this way cannot be to give a cause.

It is not, however, sufficient to claim that such explanations involve only redescription since many descriptions involve a reference to a cause. An object which appears to be a piece of rock is picked up, but on examination it is seen to be the fossil of an ammonite. Though this is a normal description it gives the cause of the object's shape. Equally, to classify a rock as sedimentary or igneous is to say something about its origin, but it is also to describe it.

Consider the following artificial example. Suppose some holes in the leaves of a plant are caused by snails eating them, and some are caused by caterpillars eating them. Let us suppose that there is a recognisable difference between the two sorts of holes, and that the hole of snails come to be called snoles and the holes of the caterpillars catoles. I might describe a hole I come across as a snole and then add that snoles are caused by snails. In one sense this would be tautologous, since to say that something is a snole is to say that it is caused by a snail. There is a logical connection between the description of what is to be explained, the snole, and what explains it, the snail eating the leaf. But in another sense it could be claimed that the fact that snoles are caused by snails gives us a piece of causal information. Snoles may be identified by their visual characteristics and the sentence 'snoles are caused by snails' is used to say that those holes which have the given visual characteristics, and as a result are called snoles, are caused by snails. What seems to be a logical connection may represent a genuine causal statement. To decide that the description of a hole as a snole is a correct description is to give a why-explanation. I see no reason to think that the same difficulties might not also apply to cases where the explanation is of an action.

If Melden's claim is that explanations by reasons are redescriptions and thus what-explanations, he must show that these redescriptions are not ones which involve a reference to a cause or some other antecedent factor, and that they do not thus provide a why-explanation. He must also show that they are not redescriptions of another type, that they are not conceptually connected with the original descriptions. In explaining that this improvident action is one in which the agent fails to take due thought for the future, what is being explained is not the object of the description but the description itself, and the logical connection holds only between the descriptions.[8] Of course to someone who did not understand the word 'improvident' to explain its meaning might make the action intelligible. But that is not the kind of explanation which, for instance, an intention provides.

If one feature of an action—Rebecca's standing up—is mentioned in saying which action is in need of an explanation, and another feature—Rebecca's intending to get a better view—is mentioned in the explanation, then these two features can only be contingently connected. Clearly the logical connection argument is not concerned with the connection between alternative descriptions but with the connection between what is described in the different ways. In fact the term 'logical' is a misnomer since it relates to links between concepts or statements, rather than between the objects, events or actions to which they apply.

III—*Must reasons be internal to actions?*

Before trying to examine further what the nature of this connection may be, let me return to Melden's arguments for saying that reasons or desires are not states or events which are antecedent to—or otherwise independent of—the actions they explain, but are rather internal to the action. Wanting, he claims, is not 'having an impression—some tension, itch, twitch or whatever'.[9] It is not by means of such a feeling or impression that different wants can be distinguished, but rather by their objects. Melden is right in suggesting that wants are not some kind of Humean impression. But it does not follow that they cannot be antecedent events. Not all conscious events are Humean impressions, and within a process of deliberation there are conscious events which are not of such a kind, are antecedent to the action, and participate in the origination of the action.

If no reference to the agent's deliberation is required in the full explanation of an action, then that deliberation can make no difference to the action itself and the way the intention is formed has nothing to do with the agent acting with that intention. In that case the action cannot be deliberative. If the action is deliberative the agent has formed his reasons prior to his action, and he can form a reason and yet not act on it. The having of a reason and acting on it seem to be independent.

Before examining the way Melden's argument applies to deliberative actions, let me look more closely at the alleged interdependence of reasons and actions when the actions are immediate. I shall assume that for these actions Melden is right in saying that the reason is simply the intention which informs the action. To state the intention is, he alleges, to describe the action, to find the correct description of the action. But what is it that makes the description correct? What is being said about the action when we say what the agent's intention was in doing it? It cannot be simply that the action is one which would fulfil that intention. Nor can the description of an action in terms of its intention be a description of the same sort as one which reports an observation.

Consider Melden's example[10] of the driver raising his arm. To give the motive, he claims, is to give a fuller characterisation of the action. When Bernard Bissett raises his arm an observer may be uncertain about what he is doing. To be told that he wants to signal or has the intention of signalling will make it clearer. But such an observer may not be uncertain. He may claim that Bernard is signalling whatever he wants or intends; his act has the characteristic conventionally understood as signalling and thus does not depend for what it is on his intention. To ascribe an intention of signalling to him is to say more than that he has signalled.

With many, but not all, of the ways of describing actions there is an element of intention built in and the contrast in the signalling example cannot be obtained. Nevertheless an action can have all the elements of such an intentional characteristic, except that intentional element. To say that Bill hurt Kathy may only be to say that Kathy was hurt as a result of what Bill did; alternatively it may also be to say that Bill intended to hurt Kathy.

Every action has many characteristics: some of these are unknown to the agent, and are clearly not part of his intention; some are known to the agent but are incidental to his doing the action—these may or may not be said to be intended, but again are not strictly part of his intention; others are known to the agent, provide the reason for his doing the action and constitute his intention. What is being said about the last set of characteristics that is not said about the other two sets? Surely the agent's attitude towards the feature must be involved. Since the agent can have a favourable attitude towards a feature without it providing the reason or intention for the acting, it looks as if the attitude has to be such that it is the having of the attitude which leads to the action being done. He has a feature-want towards the feature mentioned in the intention and does the action because of that feature-want. If it is claimed that Bernard Bissett's intention in raising his arm is to signal, and not to indicate a point of interest in the scenery, then it is not sufficient to say that he has a feature-want directed towards signalling; he might have that without his intention being to signal. Thus the action and the intention appear to be separable; without there being some additional link between the two the intention does not explain the action. For Davidson the link is given by the intention being the cause; for me the link is that the feature mentioned in the intention is favourably evaluated. To give an agent's intention may be to redescribe the action if it points out a previously unmentioned feature of it; but to say that this feature constitutes the agent's intention is to go beyond redescription because the intention is distinct from the action.

Is there any way in which Melden can resist this? Clearly his point would be that there can be no such prior attitude to act as a cause because there are no antecedent mental events or states of mind to be identified. The intention is not a prior event. To say that the agent did the action because of an intention is to say something about the action, because there is only the agent's doing of the action. The intention cannot be independent of the action. To give the agent's intention is just one more description and not a description which refers to antecedents or to consequences, but a description of an internal characteristic of the action. But this is not wholly satisfactory. It does not give sufficient grounds for picking out one of several characteristics as giving the intention. A distinction like that between a *prima facie* reason and the agent's reason (Chapter VIII, Section II) is required.

What are we to say about the cases where an action is unintended? I intended to put on the brake, but my foot slipped and as a result I accelerated. Now the intention was not a prior event if, as would usually be the case in such an example, there had been no time for thought. Thus I can have such an intention without doing an action which would have fulfilled it. So with any action which I do and for which I had an intention it is possible for me to have had the same intention without having done the action. This is not necessarily to say that having the intention must have been a prior event. We can accept that intentions are parts of actions without having to say there is anything other than a contingent connection between the intention and the action. The evidence of immediate actions suggests that intentions and, in the same way, reasons are internal to the actions, but are nevertheless independent. Though a reason may give a what-explanation of an action, it also gives a why-explanation. The action not only is done with an intention, it is done because of that action. The explanation of the immediate action must be in terms of one of the action's features rather than another being intended. (See Chapter XI, Section II for further discussion of immediate actions.)

IV—*Evaluation and the connection between reasons and actions*

The argument of this chapter suggests that in the case of immediate actions the reasons are internal to the action, while in the case of deliberative actions the reasons are formed prior to the action. Does this mean that reasons must operate in different ways in the two types of actions? To show that it does not and to bring out the point of importance indicated by the logical connection argument, I must return to some of the points made earlier, especially in Chapter VII, about the relation between feature-wants, their evaluation and the actions which follow.

When an agent deliberates, he either forms and evaluates or just evaluates his feature-wants. Those to which he gives most weight form the basis of a conclusion about how to act. He has in this way formed his reason for doing an action of a certain sort. His deciding that the feature-want is to be his reason is what leads to his action. He forms the reason prior to his action. However, until the point at which he acts he can always revise that decision—he can re-evaluate his feature-wants. In explaining his action in terms of the reason he formed in his deliberation, it is implied that he has not revised the conclusion he reached and that he is still committed to the evaluations he made. The forming of a conclusive reason for an action at one time in no way necessitates doing it; nor does it in itself explain acting on that conclusion at a later time. What needs to be added is that the agent has not changed his evaluation and that what he decided to be his reason is still his reason at the time of action. In so far as the action is the result of his having a reason for doing it, it is the result of his having the reason at the time of the action and not at an earlier time. Thus the agent must have the reason when he acts; the reason is internal to it and cannot be taken as a prior event. A similar argument can be formulated for intentions. To explain an action in terms of the agent's reasons is to explain it in terms of the reason he has in acting, however those reasons were formed. This is not, of course, to deny that the way the reasons were formed is not essential to that explanation; it is only to indicate that the reasons which explain and in whose formation we are interested are the reasons the agent had in acting.

Melden is right in claiming that intentions and reasons are internal to all intentional actions whether deliberative or immediate. It does not follow, however, that they are not independent of the action. It is contingent that an action has a non-intentional characteristic X and at the same time the characteristic of being intentionally X, though the latter characteristic explains its having the former. The intention or reason and the action are not logically connected.

X
Are Reasons Causes?

I—The origination of voluntary and involuntary actions
Most accounts of the way reasons explain make a clear-cut distinction between reasons being and not being causes. I find the distinction far from clear and find it difficult to commit myself to one or other view. Part of the difficulty lies in the concept of causality itself and part in the complex relation which reasons have to action. Valuable though it would be, I cannot hope to provide a full discussion of causality here. The concept I shall use is one which I take to conform with common sense, and one in which a cause not only precedes an effect, but is also in some sense responsible or partly responsible for that effect taking place; the cause is that which produces or brings about the effect. Any regularity view such as Hume's,[1] or the more sophisticated version of Braithwaite,[2] is too restricted; it makes it only too easy to show that reasons are not causes.[3] At the other extreme a view which makes all explanation—or at least all why-explanations—causal by definition seems to me to be too broad. Mackie characterises a cause by means of what he calls an INUS condition, so that a cause is 'an *insufficient* but *necessary* part of a condition which is itself *unnecessary* but *sufficient* for the result'.[4] Pressing the button on the television set is the cause of the picture appearing, since pressing the button, while not on its own sufficient, is necessary in the circumstances if a picture is to be obtained, and pressing the button together with the other necessary factors is sufficient to obtain a picture, but not the only possible way. I am sympathetic to this view, though it is open to criticism,[5] and I shall make use of it, even if not keeping strictly to it. My own usage is intended to be close to what I take to be usually found in common sense. I allow not only that the wind can be the cause of this shrub dying, that a lack of vitamin C causes scurvy and that my car's pinking is caused by the

timing being faulty, but also that the manager's decision was the cause of the strike, that lack of parental support is a cause of poor reading performance and that an alcoholic's desire for a drink is the cause of his breaking into the off-licence. I do not allow, however, that if Jacob's reason for going to a party is that he wants to meet a friend then that want must on conceptual grounds alone be the cause of his going to the party. I want to suggest that there is a difference between certain factors—such as desires—causing an action and those factors bringing about the action, but mediated through the deliberation of the agent. Since my concern is not centrally with whether reasons are to be called causes, but with understanding the nature of the explanations given by reasons, I hope that my argument will not be seriously undermined by failing to provide an extended account of causality.

Various candidates for the causes of actions may be found: physiological events; motives, desires or wants; external physical events; actions of the agent or of others; social or other environmental conditions; decisions or choices of the agent. To give a complete explanation of any action, instances of many of these—and also of many other factors—would have to be mentioned. Any action is the result of many different influences, whether it is determined or free. It may be argued that some of these factors are only relevant to the explanation of bodily movements, since bodily movements are different from actions and their explanations different in kind. I reject such a view. Most actions require bodily movements, and a total explanation of an action must include an explanation of the bodily movement used in the action. I shall return to this in Chapter XII. Explanations may be of a different type according to which items from the above list are mentioned and it may in the end turn out that some explanations are not causal while others are. To discuss this it is necessary to look more fully at actions which are not voluntary, are undoubtedly caused and yet are intentional.

Sam Buchanan and Victoria Adams are each told, while apparently under hypnosis, to open a window at some future time; in fact unknown to everyone else Victoria has not been successfully hypnotised. At the specified time each of them appears to do what they were told. Sam does it as a result of the hypnotist's instructions, even though he tries to rationalise his action. The hypnotist's command is the cause of his opening the window. We may not know how the causal relation works in this case or what is the mechanism by which hypnosis works, and may even have doubts about whether it does work, but it is conceivable that actions can result from hypnotic suggestion. What is implied by saying that the action is caused in this way? The implication is that what made the difference as to whether Sam opened the window or not was the hypnotist's command, and the opening of the window was a necessary consequence of that command, as long as there were no other changes in the accompanying conditions. We assume a pattern of background conditions which are no different in this situation than in others; for instance, the agent is physically capable of opening the window, the window can be opened, and so on. We then contrast Sam's case with a hypothetical case in which no command had been given to him, but all other circumstances are the same. If we claim that the hypnotist's command is the cause, then we are implying that in the hypothetical case the window would not have been opened. The command is not sufficient on its own, but is a necessary member of the group of factors which were sufficient, though not perhaps necessary, to bring about the opening of the window. It thus satisfies the criterion for an INUS condition.

Victoria's case is different; she pretends to have been hypnotised and is aware of what the hypnotist has said. In order to deceive others, she chooses at the appropriate time to open her window. In her case, as in Sam's, she would not have opened the window unless the hypnotist had told her to. Both Sam and Victoria know what they are doing in opening the windows and their actions are intentional. However, Victoria deliberates, while Sam does not, or if he does it has no effect on his action. Does the hypnotist's command to Victoria also satisfy the criteria for an INUS condition? It is in itself not sufficient, but without it she would not have opened the window and so it is necessary. Was it together with the other conditions sufficient, though not necessary, to bring about the action? This depends on what is included in the conditions. The command together with the other conditions obtaining in Sam's case are not sufficient. If the fact that she deliberated and reached the decision she did is added to the conditions, then they may be sufficient. At the very least the command must be a cause in a different way for her than for Sam.

Before pursuing this case further, let me look at the case of an alcoholic, Margaret Johnson. Her desire for alcohol causes her to have a drink and thus causes her to take the various steps necessary in order to get the drink. Len Bateman, who does not have such a compulsion, also has a desire for something alcoholic and has a drink in order to satisfy it. In both cases their desires might seem to be the cause of their having a drink. Without the desire neither agent would have one; the desire is again a necessary member of a set of seemingly sufficient conditions. Margaret's desire is irresistible, and, together with other factors, is sufficient. These other factors, such as the availability of a drink and being fit enough to get to wherever the drink is, are independent.

Len's case is different. He could have chosen not to have the drink, and if it is said that his desire caused his action, then it must do so in a different way. To make the difference we can point to the fact that the conditions which are sufficient to produce Margaret's action are not sufficient to produce the same action in his case. We must add that Len chose to satisfy his desire and could have chosen not to. Does this suggest that we differentiate both in these cases and in Sam's and Victoria's by adding an additional causal factor in explaining Len's and Victoria's actions? In their cases not only is the command or desire a cause but also their choosing to obey the command or satisfy the desire is also a cause, while in Margaret's and Sam's there are no acts of choosing to be causes.

The distinction may be made clearer by using my account of feature-wants. With Sam and Margaret the factors which are said to be causes act directly on the agent to produce the actions. The feature-wants which originate the actions are both caused and themselves directly cause the actions. Victoria and Len, however, take account of the factor in question; they have the capacity to evaluate their respective feature-wants and to decide whether they constitute sufficient reasons for acting. Victoria has a feature-want directed towards obeying the command and, though that feature-want may itself be caused, whether or not she acts on it depends on the way she evaluates it or the importance she decides to attach to its satisfaction. Thus the further condition required for Len's and Victoria's actions to take place, which is not required for Sam's and Margaret's actions, is that Len and Victoria evaluate the relevant feature-wants highly enough to act on them. An important point, discussed in Chapter IX, is that the evaluation can only be provisional until the action is taking place. Len can change his evaluation of his desire for a drink. If he does not change it, then he is continuing to hold to his evaluation and the commitment implicit in it; only when acting does his evaluation become irrevocable.

Is there any difference in type between the sets of conditions for actions which are voluntary and those for actions which are not? Is it just that in the voluntary actions there are additional conditions of the same kind as the shared conditions? I do not think so. The additional conditions depend on some of the shared conditions. It is difficult to see how one can evaluate a desire highly without having the desire. One way of putting it is to say that the additional conditions are second-order; another is to say that they are not conditions at all and are better described as qualifications of the conditions specifying the feature-wants, which make the latter conditions different in cases where so qualified from those in which they are not.

Whether or not these additional conditions are of the same order, there is still a problem of distinguishing between the explanations of different types of action. If reasons are causes, then a desire and a belief which constitute a reason cause the action they explain. If an action is explained by reasons it is voluntary, as in Len's case. But Margaret's action is also explained by a similar desire and belief, and no distinction between the explanations of the two actions is possible. The only way to preserve a causal account of reasons is to maintain that the additional conditions required for voluntary actions are causal conditions, and that an action explained by a reason is caused by the agent's desire and belief when evaluated sufficiently highly.

II—Are evaluations the causes of actions?

What at first sight seems to be a similar difficulty is raised by Davidson when he discusses ways of distinguishing between two actions, both of which result from similar desires and beliefs, but one of which is voluntary and the other accidental.

> Beliefs and desires that would rationalize an action if they caused it in the *right* way . . . may cause it in other ways. If so, the action was not performed with the intention that we could have read off from the attitudes that caused it. What I despair of spelling out is the way in which attitudes must cause actions if they are to rationalize the action.[6]

Davidson uses the following example to make the point clear.

> A climber might want to rid himself of the weight and danger of holding another man on a rope, and he might know that by loosening his hold on the rope he could rid himself of the weight and danger. This belief and want might so unnerve him as to cause him to loosen his hold, and yet it might be the case that he never *chose* to loosen his hold, nor did he do it intentionally.[7]

If a causalist such as Davidson holds that desires and beliefs are the causes of intentional and voluntary actions, he has to find a way of distinguishing between not only voluntary and involuntary actions, but intentional and unintentional actions which all result from similar desires and beliefs. Davidson admits he has not found such a way; nor does Goldman[8] seem to be more successful. The account I have given does, at first sight, seem to be an improvement. Let me distinguish two different interpretations of what happened to the climber. In A he loosens his grip unintentionally, but as a result of the belief and the want. In B he loosens his grip intentionally because of the same belief and want, and after deliberating. According to my account, in A the belief and the want cause the action; in B the belief and the want are not sufficient to cause the action, and in order to constitute the climber's reason, he has to evaluate them sufficiently highly to outweigh his evaluation of any other conflicting *prima facie* reasons.

A causalist might claim that the agent's evaluation was a cause and thus argue that my view was consistent with explanations by reasons being a form of causal explanation. Unfortunately the difficulties cannot be solved so simply. It may be that the climber does deliberate about what he wants, and ends up evaluating his desire more highly than any conflicting desires. As a result he becomes nervous, his hand shakes and he loosens his hold. His evaluating his desire highly is the cause of his action, and yet he did not act intentionally. This shows that in the case of an intentional action performed for a reason, it is not enough either to say that the agent's desire is the cause of his action or that his evaluation of the desire is the cause of his action.

This is a difficulty not simply for a causalist who cannot make the required distinctions; it is also one for my account, since it is equally important for me to distinguish between actions in which the agent's evaluating causes an accidental action and actions in which the agent's evaluating leads to the agent acting on that evaluation. Before trying to deal with this, I want to follow up another possible line of criticism.

III—*The evaluation of reasons and the possibility of an infinite regress*

There is an argument which suggests that all actions must be caused, whether or not they are explained by reasons, to which my account seems particularly vulnerable. If an evaluation is necessary for an agent to act on reasons, then that act of evaluation in which the agent gives weight to certain factors must, it is alleged, be caused. If it is not, there appears to be an infinite regress. This criticism has been well expressed in the following terms.[9] For an agent to perform action A deliberately he must not only do so for reasons R; the beliefs and desires which go to make up R must be such that he has turned them into reasons, and his action A_1 of turning them into reasons must not be causally explicable. He must have performed A_1 deliberatively, *i.e.* for reasons R_1, and he must have chosen R_1 himself; and so on.

How can this argument be met? First of all, let me agree that in some cases in which an agent appears to evaluate the weight he gives to various factors may be caused; in such a case the agent does not truly evaluate. Let me also reject a rather sophistical way of dealing with it in which giving weight and evaluating are said not to be true actions and thus cannot themselves be the result of deliberation in the same way as the action they lead to. Rather I want to suggest that though an evaluation may be supported by reasons it may not be, without thereby becoming arbitrary or having to be caused.

Bridget Macdonald is driving her car when she sees someone who is walking alone suddenly collapse. She stops the car and goes over; she sees he needs help and after some deliberation and effort gets him into her car and drives him to the nearest hospital. She has a passenger with her whom she was taking shopping and who asks Bridget why she behaved as she did. Bridget replies, no doubt rather crossly, that she wanted to save unnecessary pain and suffering, thus suggesting that this was the want she evaluated most highly. The question of what her reason was in making that evaluation seems absurd. It does not need a reason, and the absence of such a reason does not imply that she was caused to evaluate that way. She could give value to the want because of the nature of the want and not because of any other factor associated with the want or its object. She decides it is to have value. It is not arbitrary because of the absence of a reason: it does not need a reason.

What would be involved if an evaluation were caused? It is possible to imagine a case in which, as a result of certain processes of conditioning, an agent appears to evaluate a factor in a particular way, though it is difficult to know how this would show itself. Is such an agent really evaluating? Certainly the factor he is supposed to be evaluating carries a certain weight in his deliberation, and that it does so is caused. But he does not give it that weight; it comes like some impulse-desires with a weight already attached (see Chapter VII, Section II). Thus the weight it has is not the result of his evaluation, and he cannot have evaluated. The concept of evaluation as I have tried to develop it excludes the possibility that what is done in evaluating is caused. If it is caused, it is not evaluation.

IV—Reasons are not causes

I have considered and rejected various factors which might constitute the cause of an action explained by reasons: the desire and the belief which constitute the reason; the evaluation of the desire and the belief which turns them into a reason; an event or process which causes that evaluation. None of these seems to work, and yet there still remains the problem of differentiating between a case in which the agent's evaluation causes an unintentional action and a case in which the agent's evaluation is the ground of the agent doing the same action intentionally.

Let me return to the conclusion which I drew from the logical connection argument (Chapter IX, Section IV). There I argued that the agent's reason and thus his evaluation of his desire and belief, though formed prior to the action it explained, must nevertheless be part of the action. This is because an agent can always revise his evaluation until he acts on it. It is only in the action that the agent commits himself finally to the desire and the belief being his reason. In the light of this let us consider again Davidson's climber and compare interpretation B with interpretation A, when it is his evaluation which makes him loosen his grip. In A, though he has made a judgment of value, he has not given effect to it in action; it is still only a provisional evaluation. He has not decided finally on it; if he had, he would be acting on it. He is not acting on it; rather the provisional evaluation at the stage it has reached has an effect on him which leads to his grip loosening. The desire and the belief have not been finally evaluated, since he has not acted on them. It is not possible to tell what his final evaluation would have been if his unintentional action had not taken place. Thus there are two possibilities: the climber has completed his evaluation and thus must be acting on it—he loosens his grip; or the loosening of the climber's grip is caused by the evaluating he has done so far, and his evaluation is not complete. In the first case he acts for a reason, and in doing so commits himself to the evaluation implicit in it; neither the desire and the belief which are evaluated nor the evaluation itself can cause his action, except in the sense that without them he would not have acted. They are not themselves events, actions or states separable from the action they explain, even though they are not logically connected with the action.

No doubt there are examples in which physical causes have to be concurrent with the effects they produce; certainly to suppose a cause must be antecedent to its effect leads to difficulties about the time-gap between them. But it is not just the concurrence of the explanatory factor with what it explains which makes explanations by reasons different from causal explanations. It is also the nature of the evaluation and its relation to action; it is the very nature of agency and that needs far more consideration.

I reject the claim that reasons are logically connected with the actions they explain, and that reasons are not concerned with the origination of actions. Reasons do provide why-explanations, and are necessary to what they explain taking place. This might suggest that reasons provide a form of causal explanation. On the other hand, they explain in a different way from causes and are connected with what they explain in a different way. These differences are important and need emphasising. For this reason, even though I am reluctant to take sides in the argument, my sympathies lie more with those who say that reasons are not causes than with those who say they are.

XI
Non-deliberative Actions

I—Different types of non-deliberative actions
So far the discussion has been mainly of actions resulting from deliberation. In these cases the reasons have arisen within the deliberation and have been formulated by the agent. However, many actions occur without any process of deliberation taking place or without the deliberation having any effect on what is actually done. For some of these it would be inappropriate to give reasons in explaining them; for others the natural form of the explanation would be in terms of reasons. The latter are the subject of this chapter.

Non-deliberative actions which are explained in terms of reasons are of various different types. Firstly, there are those where action takes place on the spur of the moment and either there is no time for thought or thought is not taken: a cat runs in front of the car, so I brake suddenly; a child cries and her father hits her violently. Secondly, there are every day actions which do not require thought; we know what we are doing but do not think about it or of doing anything else: as I talk, I take a drink from my cup of coffee. Thirdly, there are habitual actions where a very definite pattern of action is being repeated: I wind my watch whenever I take it off. Fourthly, there are actions for which we have reasons we are not aware of, but they have not been repressed and can readily be brought to mind and thus are—using Freud's term[1]—pre-conscious reasons: I buy a book, thinking I want to read it, but in fact because I want to impress my guests. Fifthly, there are actions for which we have unconscious reasons, reasons we are not aware of, have repressed and cannot readily bring to mind: I am rude not because I want to offend, but because of a deep-seated fear of any close relationship. These groupings are not exclusive: for instance, an account of some unconscious reasons may be given in terms of habits; nor are the groupings exhaustive. However,

I think they cover most of the significant cases of non-deliberative actions for which reasons are given and an account of them will signpost the way towards the provision of an account of any other kinds. It is not possible to be comprehensive or systematic, or to outline any general features which an account of the explanations of such actions must have. But there are various types of ground on which we can attribute reasons to these actions. I shall try to indicate what some of these are and show that the account I have given for deliberative actions can be applied to these.

At first sight it may look as if the concept of reason which I have outlined for deliberative actions cannot work for immediate actions and that two different and independent concepts of reason are needed for each type of action. Alternatively, it may be argued that this appearance is misleading, and that there are strong connections between the ways 'reason' is used in connection with each. Or again, it might be claimed that with non-deliberative actions the use of the term 'reason' is misleading, and that all such explanations are causal in the narrower sense of the term which for some excludes explanations by reasons.

The last of these should be immediately rejected. Certainly some actions for which reasons are given do in fact require a causal explanation of the kind mentioned. But this is not true of all non-deliberative actions. It is common to talk of such actions in terms of reasons, and it seems to help in understanding them. This kind of action would rightly be described in terms of what the agent does, and in most cases in terms of what he does voluntarily, rather than in terms of what happens to him. Many actions for which there are unconscious reasons seem voluntary, because the agent has a purpose of his own in doing them and could have chosen other actions; to say of one such action that the agent does not know why he did it and does not accept its explanation does not imply that he has not chosen it rather than something else. Even if such actions are not voluntary, it is still the case that there are strong resemblances between them and other actions which are voluntary, both in themselves and in the way they are explained. Thus for many of these actions a straightforward causal account seems wrong, and an attempt must be made to give an account of reasons which will accommodate them. There is less to choose between the other two possible ways of dealing with non-deliberative actions. However, the second of them seems to me preferable and I shall take the different uses of 'reason' as connected. In the rest of the chapter I shall try to show what these connections are and that a use for the concept of reason in non-deliberative actions can be derived from the suggested use for deliberative action. Without understanding the use of the concept for the latter actions it would for the most part be impossible to understand its use for the former actions.

II—Immediate actions

Let me begin with immediate actions—those which belong to the first two of the five groupings. (See Chapter IX, Section III for earlier discussion of these.) In some cases the agent seems to reason without realising it; it happens so quickly that he does not notice the whole of the process at the time, though later he may recognise something as having occurred in his reasoning. It may be difficult to verify whether a thought has actually been part of such a process, but certainly we sometimes feel a sense of familiarity with an idea or thought and suppose, therefore, that is must have occurred before in our thinking, and this is evidence—even if not very good evidence—for its having been involved in our decision-making. But this suggestion cannot plausibly be generalised to say that in any immediate action the reason must have been part of a process of deliberation which went unnoticed by the agent.

To try and arrive at an alternative account let me consider the example of Barbara Simmons: she is driving along steadily and calmly when suddenly she brakes hard and frightens her passenger. Let us suppose that it is appropriate to ask for her reason. She claims that she was trying to avoid a cat which ran out on to the road. She gives this as her reason and it indicates what her intention was in braking. Her action is immediate and forethought was impossible.

The reason cannot, it seems, refer to anything which occurred before the action and must be coincidental with or even a part of the action. Equally, a judgment involved cannot be prior to the action; rather in acting the agent is making a judgment.

Two of the characteristics of Barabara Simmons' action are avoiding the cat and frightening her passenger, and the first is picked out as providing her reason. What is being claimed about it when it is so picked out? In such cases what is meant by saying something is her reason? It might be suggested that her reason is one of wanting to avoid the cat because her action is what she would have done if she had formed the intention of avoiding it. But the action would also satisfy an intention of frightening her passenger. We cannot therefore infer a reason from seeing what intentions are fulfilled. Nor is it sufficient to say that not only would the action satisfy this intention, but that this intention is the one most consistent with her past character and past ways of acting. Though her character may provide evidence for her reasons and intentions it cannot be the basis of what is meant by her reason, because it is always possible for any agent to act for a reason—or with an intention—which is out of character.

Another suggestion is that what is meant by the agent's reason is whatever justifies her action or provides a good reason for doing such an action, either for anyone in general or for anyone who shares her known beliefs; again, though providing evidence, the reference to justification is not acceptable, because the suggested reasons may not have been the agent's justification. Moreover the kind of reason suggested must be inferred, and while that may be all that an observer can do, it is not all that an agent can do even in an immediate action. In many such cases, though she can see that it is possible to find a reason which justifies the action, she cannot permit herself the comfort of relying on that to explain her action.

Is it possible that the reason is internal to the action and yet is something to do with the agent's thinking or state of mind? In many immediate actions the reason may be identified with the agent's intention, and I will therefore consider this possibility in terms of intentions. To give an agent's intention we pick out one of the characteristics of the action which unless the intention is unconscious, she must be aware of in acting and to which she has a special attitude.

Barbara Simmons may be aware both that she is avoiding the cat and that she is frightening her passenger, but her attitudes to each are different. She wants to avoid the cat, and though she may want to frighten her passenger she is not braking because of that want. This is not to say that she first forms the want and then makes a decision to satisfy it. The want is simultaneous with the action; in acting, she is wanting. She knows what she is doing and what she wants to do in doing it. She evaluates the feature to which her want is directed, and gives it such importance that she does an action which has that feature. She may later regret her action, the intention and the evaluation which went with it, but nevertheless at the time of the action and without prior thought she did evaluate in that way. She did not do it after deliberation but made an immediate judgment of importance. It is this judgment which attaches to one characteristic or feature and not to any others, and this enables us to say that the feature provides her intention and her reason. Such a judgment can be immediate, and needs no prior thought or indeed formulation separate from the action. In acting she thinks she is so judging, though she may be mistaken, just as she may be mistaken about her intention or her reason.

Does this account apply to impulsive actions—to actions the agent does not think about, though he could have? Frank Jones can stand his child's crying no longer and without thinking hits her violently. His reason for his action is that he wants to stop her crying. To talk of evaluation in such a context is inappropriate, but not because it would be a wrong way to evaluate. Rather it is because there is no evaluation of the want, and from almost any point of view, whether moral or prudential, there should have been. What we criticise in the action is not his wanting to stop the child crying, but his failure to control that want. He has allowed his impulse-desire to determine his action, even though he could have controlled it. His action is explained in terms of his want, and that constitutes his reason. He could have formed other feature-wants or given greater weight to other feature-wants he already had, and did not do so.

I do not claim that these ways of dealing with the two cases will apply to all actions done immediately or on impulse, but they cover many of the cases of such actions in which the agent rightly thinks he knows what he is doing.

III—*Habitual actions*

Some actions which might be thought to be immediate do not fit in with the account I have just given; in these we act automatically without noticing what we are doing, and yet the actions are intentional. Some at least of these are the product of habits, and we can only explain such actions by reference to these habits. I shall now try to show how such explanations can be fitted into the account of reasons I have given.

Habits are more complex and varied than they seem to be. There are fixed and definite habits, specific both in what triggers off the habit and in the actions which result from the habit. Whenever William takes off his watch, he winds it. Here we have a definite action which is repeated whenever a particular situation recurs. There are other habits in which the situations which stimulate the habit are very varied, although they will all have one feature in common and it is that feature which gives rise to the habitual response. With some habits these responses will be specified; with others they will be very varied, though all will have a common feature. An example of the former would be Philip always reacting to being asked a question by putting his arms behind his back; an example of the latter would be Basil's habitual rudeness to women he dislikes. In each of these last two cases new and very different contexts may occur; in the former Philip responds with a definite and specific action; in the latter it seems as if no particular action is suggested since rudeness may take many different forms; all that happens is that whatever other characteristics Basil's action has it has that of rudeness. In fact in all three examples the features which either trigger off the habit or are shared by the habitual responses differ in degree and not in kind. Taking off his watch is only one feature of the otherwise varied situations in which William takes off his watch, but it does seem to be a feature which is more easily isolated and which stands out more clearly than a feature such as that of being asked a question. There are many more different ways of being asked a question than of taking off one's watch. Equally Philip's and Basil's responses differ in the extent to which they are specific.

Are habits simply dispositions or tendencies to act in particular ways? Dispositions seem to suggest no more than some degree of regularity in actions. However, with habits there is more than regularity. Someone may be said to have a disposition or tendency to be punctual, but this does not need to be the result of habit. He may choose and even deliberate each time and this would not make it any the less true that he has such a tendency. Whether or not it constitutes a disposition may be arguable, but it is quite clear that in the case of someone who deliberates and chooses it would be a mistake to call this regularity of behaviour a habit; a habit suggests that the action is unconsidered, and that in so far as the action conforms to a habit it is automatic. If I am trying to establish a habit, say, in my golf swing then I am trying to achieve a state in which I swing the golf-club in the right way without having to give it any thought. Until that is accomplished my swing is not the result of habit.

An habitual response may be of different kinds: it may be an action or it may be a feeling, an emotion or an attitude. In the latter case we may still call the action which results habitual even though it is in fact the feeling or attitude the action expresses which is habitual. Some habits, such as a good golf swing, may be established deliberately. Some may be the result of a traumatic experience: an incident may result in overwhelming emotion such as fear, guilt or shame and, as a consequence, whenever the feature of the incident with which the emotion was associated recurs the same emotion also recurs. Some habits may be said to be the result of chance in so far as there is no obvious or significant reason for having acquired the habit.

To explain an habitual action may be to give the stimulus-feature or the response-feature; it may be to give the reason why the agent deliberately formed the habit or to say why the habit was formed without the agent even being aware of it; it may be to give the purpose achieved by the habit, or to say what function the habit has; it may be to say what were the grounds for the agent not restraining his habit. Though any of these explanations may be phrased in terms of reasons, they are not all explanations by reasons. Those which are legitimately expressed in terms of reasons cannot refer, as they did in the case of immediate actions, to what the agent had in mind at the time of acting.

Let me refer again to William who habitually winds his watch. Why is he winding it? He always does so when he takes it off. Though this gives a partial explanation and may make his action intelligible, it does not give his reason. An alternative answer might be that it prevents the watch stopping. Though William may not actually think of this before or even when winding his watch—he may not even realise that he is winding it—it is a good reason for winding a watch. But it does not follow that it is *his* reason. It would only constitute his reason if it had been the reason why he had formed the habit, or if on finding he had the habit it was his reason for maintaining it or for not trying to break it. To say this seems to suggest that deliberation did occur at some time or other. Certainly in those habitual actions where deliberation does take place, even if not at the time of the action, it is from the deliberation that we derive the reasons.

At the opposite extreme there are actions where the habit is so strong that the agent could not act otherwise and therefore the action is caused, the cause being given by the presence of the stimulus on this occasion and the habitual connection of the stimulus and the response. Examples are nervous laughter, various mannerisms which one would avoid if one could or a sudden and uncontrollable burst of anger regularly provoked by a particular stimulus. In these cases the causal explanation is of acting from the habit, or of the maintenance of the habit. Such an explanation must be distinguished from the causal explanation of the origin of the habit. It is possible that a habit which originated in deliberation might, having been voluntarily adopted, become compulsive. Equally it is possible that a habit which originated causally might become the subject for deliberation, and only be maintained because of the reasons the agent formed within that deliberation. We have, then, a number of different kinds of explanations of habitual actions. Firstly, the explanation of the action may refer to the cause of the habit and to the habit causing the action. Secondly, it may refer to the cause of the habit and to the agent's reasons for not breaking the habit, reasons which arise from his deliberating at some time after the habit was formed. Thirdly, it may refer to the reasons the agent had in forming the habit deliberatively and to the habit causing the action. Fourthly, it may refer to reasons both for the formation of the habit and for its maintenance.

This still leaves a group of habitual actions which are not compulsive, but also do not seem to have been determined by deliberation either about the habit or the action itself; it may be that the agent has not deliberated at all or it may be that he has not made the results of his deliberation effective in influencing his actions. With the former alternative he may not even be aware of the habit, but he could have been and could have effectively deliberated about it. With the latter it may be that the agent was aware of the habit, aware that it should be restrained and that he had to give constant attention to restraining it, but nevertheless failed to give that attention though he could have done so. Carol Chatterton tries very hard to guard her tongue because she tends to say far more than she would wish when provoked. She fails to notice a particular provocation because she is deeply involved in an argument, and as a result responds in her habitual way, though she immediately regrets it; if she had been paying attention to what she was saying, she could have stopped herself saying it. In such a case the action results from negligence. This is an important class of actions for which a causal explanation does not seem appropriate, because such an agent is responsible for her actions even though she does not have reasons for them of the kind I have outlined. It appears that she cannot be said to give greater weight to the other factors than to restraining her habit, because she does not think about the latter and thus about what weight to give to it. Unless we think about our habits, we find ourselves automatically acting in accordance with them. Such a person as Carol Chatterton tries to think about them, but on this occasion fails to do so because of her involvement in the argument. Her negligence is explained by the weight she is giving to other factors, or by the fact that she has not given the weight she could have to restraining her habit.

What I want to suggest in such cases is that habits may be factors acting directly on the agent and affecting his action without being mediated through his consciousness. They need not be the only factors doing so; physical constraints may also act on him. As I shall argue in the next chapter, the presence of such factors is not incompatible with an explanation by reasons. However, in cases of the sort just discussed it is not necessary for the agent to have had any reasons; he may simply be paying no attention to what he is doing. His action must be explained in terms of the factors providing influences which he could have evaluated but did not. These factors act causally rather than as reasons, and thus we may say that there were causes for what he did but not that he was caused to act thus. To explain an action in terms of the agent's negligence is not to give reasons, but to suggest that he did not have the reasons he could have had and should have had.

I want to look now at those habits which appear to have a purpose or function, and yet are habits which happen for no reason, or happen as a result of factors of which the agent is unaware or over which he has no control. To explain an action by reference to the purpose which the habit seems to have looks like giving the agent's purpose and thus his reason. Why does Derek always scratch his ear every time he sees a dog? Why does Colin always use a certain speech mannerism? These may at first seem pointless but on looking at them further it can be claimed that scratching his ear is the way by which Derek tries to hide his fear of dogs, while

Colin's mannerism is a way of trying to show that he means what he says. Neither form of action may achieve the respective purposes, but nevertheless to discover the purpose is said to provide a reason for the agent doing the action and to make the action intelligible. I can see no grounds for claiming that these explanations of Derek's and Colin's actions give their reasons, if at no time were they aware of those purposes and could neither choose to have them nor to change them.

My conclusion at this stage is that there is a variety of habitual actions which can be explained in different ways—some by reasons, some not. In some cases the agent has reasons, though at the time of the action he may not think of them. Some of these reasons relate to the way the habits were formed and the reasons which the agent had in deliberately developing them. Some of the reasons may relate to those the agent had for maintaining the habit or for not breaking it. There are some actions which we try to explain in terms of a habit, but where the genesis or even the existence of the habit is unknown to the agent, and in such cases we should not use explanations in terms of the agent's reasons.

IV—*Unconscious reasons*

Let me now discuss those actions for which the agent is alleged to have unconscious or pre-conscious reasons. To begin with I shall deal only with the fact that the agent is not conscious of them, and for brevity's sake will refer to them as unconscious reasons the agent is not aware of or is mistaken about his reason for doing his action, but he is nevertheless alleged to have a reason. In such examples the action is what the agent would have done if he had had the reason; the action looks purposive and makes sense when a particular purpose is attributed to it. Though this is so, it can be argued that such a purpose is different in kind from one which an agent is consciously seeking to fulfil, and is closer to those which are ascribed to natural phenomena and are reducible to causes. The form of the related explanations is less like that of the explanations of deliberative actions than that of causal explanations for compulsive actions. Though in the end this seems to me close to being the right answer, I do not think it should be accepted without examining some examples of unconscious reasons. As with other nondeliberative actions it is not possible to give one account of how all such reasons work. They work in different ways, and I can only indicate some approaches to dealing with these examples.[2]

Let me start with a relatively simple example. When Geoffrey Washington is asked by Mrs. Smith for his opinion of her new hat he tells her that it does not suit her; in his eyes he does this because he believes in truth and honesty. On the other hand, an observer who knows Geoffrey well is convinced that in fact he wants to hurt Mrs. Smith because her husband has just been promoted over him and this is his unconscious reason.

It is certainly true that if he had wanted to hurt her the action would have been appropriate. But this is not enough; if the given reason is the agent's unconscious reason not only is it the case that if he had had that reason he would have acted the way he has and that he does not acknowledge the reason; it must also be the case that the agent acts *because* of this reason.

When, as an observer, I try to explain the actions of another, I have no access to anything except what he does and says and the reactions of others. I cannot always rely on his honesty in disclosing his reasons. I infer his reasons from what I see of his behaviour, and attribute to him those reasons which, given my knowledge of him and his actions, would seem best satisfied by the action. The agent may claim that his reasons are different from those I attribute to him. If those attributed are unworthy, then though they are his reasons it is understandable that he should be reluctant to accept them. His disowning of them is not a conclusive argument against their being his. However, I may be reluctant to think that the agent knows that they are his reasons and is trying to deceive me; I therefore suggest he is deceiving himself. Is this just a way of avoiding two possibilities neither of which I want to accept, even if the cost is having to accept an apparently paradoxical explanation?

Let me consider some of the ways in which self-deception[3]

Non-deliberative actions

may be possible. When Geoffrey Washington tells Mrs. Smith what he thinks of her hat he may well be aware both that what he is saying is truthful and that it will hurt. At the time of the act he may even be giving a favourable evaluation to both features. He may want both to be truthful and to hurt her. The same action will result whichever of these feature-wants is given the greater weight. He suggests to himself that he gives little weight to wanting to hurt her and much more weight to wanting to be truthful. An observer may suggest that he is mistaken and that it is the first want which has the greater weight. Is it possible for an agent to be wrong and an observer to be right about the weight a feature-want has in his deliberation? From what I said earlier it may seem that, since the weight which a feature-want has is given to it by the agent, he cannot be wrong, though he may deceive the observer. The only way he can be wrong is for the feature-wants to which he gives weight to be irrelevant to the origination of the action, and for impulse-desires over which he can have no control to lead to the action.

The situation is more complex than this and there are other ways in which the agent can be wrong. The trouble comes about mainly because of the part impulse-desires can play in an agent's deliberation. I have already mentioned some of the problems in the discussion of weakness of will (Chapter VII, Section II). An impulse-desire is a feature-want of an agent which does not result from his decision. Furthermore, its strength is not decided by him. I nevertheless suggested that an agent can evaluate an impulse-desire, can decide how much weight he is to give it. The latter judgment is the result of comparing the impulse-desire with other feature-wants he has. In making such comparisons the strength of the impulse-desire is one factor that would usually be taken into account. However, an agent may fail to realise how strong an impulse-desire is, perhaps because he does not want to realise how strong it is. Thus an impulse-desire may play a bigger part in his decision than the agent allows, because he does not want it to play a part, because he does not realise its strength or even does not realise he has it. The resulting actions may be compulsive if the impulse-desire cannot be restrained, whatever weight the agent has decided to give to it and to the opposing wants. Or they may be voluntary but still the result of an impulse-desire about the impact of which the agent is unaware and which he does not restrain even though he could. Such cases are like those of negligence; the agent could have given less weight to the feature-want but does not do so. The feature-want acts causally on him, and in the absence of his interference in the causal process leads to action.

Let me draw attention to some aspects of this account. Firstly, it is part of the concept of a feature-want, as I originally outlined it, that it leads to action unless there are competing wants. Hence if an agent such as Geoffrey Washington has a feature-want directed towards hurting Mrs. Smith, has no competing feature-wants and does not think of forming any, then he will act so as to hurt her. Secondly, in an example such as the present one, it does not need to be the case that there is only one feature-want; clearly it is possible to have other feature-wants which point in the same direction. There is then the problem of deciding which of the favourable wants is the one which carries most weight, especially when there is no need to decide about their relative weight, but only whether all the feature-wants favourable to the action carry more weight than the feature-wants which are unfavourable. The difficult cases are where there is a feature-want the agent would prefer not to have or prefer not to admit to. The only way to decide is to ask hypothetical questions about how the agent would have deliberated if he had not had one or other of the feature-wants. But this is a problem about the verification of explanations, which I shall discuss in Chapter XIII, and not about their nature. Thirdly, the account allows the possibility of an agent having a feature-want which he does not recognise. Is this consistent with my account of feature-wants? It seems to me to be so, even though, when an agent has a feature-want, he has a pro-attitude towards a possible state of affairs which is sufficient to motivate him to act so as to bring about that state of affairs. For there is nothing in any of these conditions which suggests that the agent must be aware of having a pro-attitude or aware that it is sufficient to motivate him. I would agree that, when formulating the conditions, I had in mind those cases in which the agent is aware of his feature-wants; much more needs to be said about the way in which feature-wants can operate when unknown to the agent. However, they can do so and this is not inconsistent with their being feature-wants.

Once these possibilities are recognised the way is open for an account of the way many sorts of unconscious feature-wants operate whether they are near the surface, and what Freud would have called pre-conscious, or deep-seated and repressed. Many of the remaining problems can be solved by framing the account in terms of habits and the way the habitual association of certain situations with particular feelings or emotions may have originated in early experiences.[4] Conditioning is one way such habits can be formed and explanations in terms of conditioning are one form of explanation by means of habits.

Freud gives a purposive account of the formation of such habits. Little Hans's phobia,[5] a fear of horses, is interpreted in terms of Hans's unconscious substitution of horses for his father as the object of his emotions, thus dealing with the conflict between his fear or hatred of his father and his love for him. This may be a useful way to understand such a phobia, but it is not difficult to interpret such unconscious purposes as feature-wants of which the agent is unaware, and this does not seem incompatible with what Freud is saying. However, it is difficult to reconcile what he says about the unconscious engaging in rational activity, as if the unconscious purposes belong to part of a process of calculation, with the account of feature-wants and reasons I have given. It is possible to give an interpretation[6] of such cases as Little Hans's which does not involve supposing that rational activity is taking place. Indeed it is possible to interpret the evidence in Little Hans's case in terms of an accidental association of experiences of horses with things his father says, or other experiences of his father. This association is not surprising. For: 'Horses interested him the most of all the large animals; playing at horses was his favourite game with the other children. I had a suspicion—and this was confirmed by Hans's father when I asked him—that the first person who had served Hans as a horse must have been his father'.[7] The transference of a feeling from the object to which it is really directed to one with which the object is associated is not puzzling. Someone, particularly a child, may feel afraid in a situation and yet not identify, or identify wrongly, what it is that gives rise to the fear; the same possibility of misidentification occurs with many other emotions or feelings.

Freud's explanation of Little Hans's phobia suggests that at the time when he began to fear horses he had an unconscious purpose in doing so; it was a way of coping with the fear or hatred he is alleged to have had for his father. Of course the story as Freud presents it is far more complex, and even if his theory is rejected his insights into the effects of the sexual attitudes of his parents on Hans must be respected. Could not these insights be perfectly consistent with an account of the origin of the habit in terms of accidental association? I do not say that such an account is wholly satisfactory, but it is not clear that the connection between the father and horses is purposive in any sense other than that in which purposive explanations are given of natural phenomena. The only way in which Little Hans could be said to have reasons is by saying that he acts *as if* he has reasons or purposes which he has chosen, in the same way as an animal may be said to act *as if* it has reasons. In fact the explanation by reasons must in this case be reduced to a causal explanation of his phobia and of the formation of his habitual response to horses.

As I said earlier there are different kinds of unconscious reasons, many of which require to be dealt with in a different way from that just suggested. The subject is important, and Freud's views about the nature of his explanation should not be lightly dismissed. I hope I have indicated, however sketchily, some of the lines along which an argument consistent with my account of reasons could be developed.

XII
Compatibility

I—Actions and bodily movements
Important though it is, deliberation plays only a small part in the origination of even deliberative actions. The agent's beliefs, whether religious, moral or ontological, his emotions and feelings, his physical make-up and capacities, his concepts and the way he organises his experience, and much else besides, provide the context in which deliberation takes place. That context affects the way he sees the situation he is in and the range of possibilities from which he chooses and the way he expresses these. Part of this context may be under his control and known to him; but much of it is not. The extent to which there are unknown factors in the context is difficult to determine, since even the most intelligent, the most open-minded and the most self-conscious observer is still limited to a lesser or greater degree by the same kind of factors as is any agent he is observing. It is easy in concentrating, as I have, on the rational aspect of action to forget how much else, whether physical or mental, conscious or unconscious, cultural or individual, is relevant to the full explanation of an action.

The reasons which correctly explain an action cannot provide the whole explanation, and those factors which are not explained seem to require a causal explanation. How can different types of explanation be compatible? There might seem to be less problem if explanations by reasons are taken to be causal explanations. But there would still be the problem of reconciling different kinds of causal explanation, especially the explanation of an action with the explanation of the bodily movement required for that action. I do not think my account of reasons gives rise to special problems; indeed it seems to me easier with this account to show how different explanations can co-exist, and to show that the possibility of sociological and psychological explanations is not ruled out by reasons.

One solution to the problem of the relation of explanations of actions to explanations of the associated bodily movements is the Kantian one[1] of two worlds, the bodily movements being part of a physical world determined by causes and the actions part of a noumenal world, self-determined and thus explained by reasons. But this merely changes the problem to one of the relation between the two worlds and how they can interact. Nor does the linguistic version of this solution help any more. To say that the concepts associated with actions belong to a different category from the concepts associated with bodily movements is true,[2] but does not help to relate an action to the bodily movement required for it.

Melden rightly says that actions are not bodily movements plus motives.[3] Actions cannot be broken down or analysed into parts which are not themselves actions. On the other hand it is possible to distinguish between different characteristics of what happens when an agent performs an action. There are well-known problems about whether different descriptions must relate to different actions,[4] but I shall not discuss them, though I believe some of them can be sidestepped by restating them in terms of different characteristics of what is happening.

To find a solution to the problems of compatibility, it is necessary to consider a wider range of characteristics than those mentioned in descriptions of actions. If an agent is observed at a particular time, the resulting description could include descriptions of his observable bodily movements, the internal workings of his body, his mental states, what he is doing in moving his body, and changes in his environment. Some of these may relate to antecedents and consequents of what is happening, and I shall exclude them from the description proper, which will relate to what the agent is doing and what is happening to him at the time in question. Thus we may describe what is happening on a certain occasion by saying that Bernard Bissett is signalling, that his arm is rising, his heart is beating, his muscles are moving in a certain way and that he has red hair. (This example was used in Chapter IX, Section III.) If our interest is in the action, then some details such as the colour of his hair are irrelevant and some, like the beating of his heart, need not be mentioned because they have nothing to do with this action being of the particular kind it is. Even in a relatively simple action, there remain many possibilities. Those which are mentioned in a particular description depend on our interests in giving such a description. If we are trying to explain why someone acted as he did and are interested in it from the agent's point of view, then we must give a description which depends on what he took himself to be doing. If our interests are in what is common to this and the actions of others, we may describe what is happening in terms which see action as occurring in a social context. If our interest is in the workings of the body we may describe what happens in physiological terms.

Alice Miller is voting in an election. Even in identifying the action a description has already been given. Other descriptions may also relate to the intentional aspect of what she is doing. She is moving her hand, putting a mark on the paper and is registering her disapproval of the present government. Or the descriptions may refer only to bodily movements: her hand is moving, her arm-muscles are undergoing certain specified changes and a particular set of impulses occurs in her brain. All of these descriptions can be simultaneously true, and an explanation can be demanded for any part of what is described as occurring. Such an explanation will show why it is that a happening with the characteristic mentioned in the description is taking place. Which description is given or which characteristic is mentioned in asking for an explanation depends on our interests, just as what explanation is given will also depend on our interests. The fact that what is happening at any one moment has a number of different characteristics means that it may have a number of different explanations, since any explanation of what is happening is an explanation of why what is happening has a certain characteristic.

We may explain much of what is happening when Alice Miller votes by referring to her intentions and what she took herself to be doing, though we may add extra elements according to the characteristic being explained: we may add an explanation of what voting is if explaining why she is marking the paper; we may add an account of her political views if explaining why she is registering her disapproval. But some of the characteristics of what is happening will be unknown to her or not be part of her intention. Some may relate to social aspects of her action, some to unconscious intentions, some to physiological processes.

For an intentional action to take place other events may have to take place, and what is happening may have to have non-intentional characteristics. In order to drive a car certain things must take place in the engine, whether or not one knows anything about what they are. To explain what is happening as a car is driven may require an explanation of the car's movement in terms of the wheels turning, the transmission-shaft revolving, and so on through the whole mechanism of the engine. Another explanation may be that Audrey wants to get from London to Birmingham and has decided to use her car for the journey, and this can in its turn be explained in terms of her reasons for wanting to get to Birmingham. The explanation of the intentional action of driving the car along the road may be given in terms of reasons, but for the action to be possible the car has to be moving and the explanations of that in terms of the mechanism of the engine and the chemical properties of petrol gives part of the explanation of what is happening, whether or not Audrey has any knowledge of mechanics or chemistry.

Just as the workings of the car-engine may be introduced into the explanation of Audrey's action, so may the workings of an agent's body be introduced into the explanation of his action. When Bernard Bissett signals he has to move his body in some way. There may be no unique bodily movement which has to occur for signalling to take place, but in any particular case of signalling some bodily movement will be involved. The bodily movement used in signalling may be used to do something quite different, and equally various means can be used to signal. Nevertheless a particular action of signalling must involve a specific bodily movement. A description of what is happening when Bernard is signalling might give his bodily movements rather than what he is doing or intending, and to explain what is happening when he signals is partly to explain these bodily movements. In whatever way we explain his signalling and explain the movements of his body in signalling, these explanations must be compatible, since they are of different characteristics of the same thing.

Let me look a little more closely at explanations of bodily movements. In explaining the bodily movement of raising the arm a causal account can be given, tracing back its origins through muscle movements to brain impulses. It may be alleged that this causal story can go back long before the signalling. If this is the case, and the story is complete in itself, then the agent's decision is irrelevant to the way his arm moved, and it would seem that contrary to appearances the bodily movement did not constitute an intentional action, and that any explanation in terms of an intentional aspect is mistaken. If the signalling is an intentional action then it is in some sense the carrying out of an intention or decision, and that means that without the intention or decision it would not have happened. It follows that the bodily movement which takes place when the agent signals would not have happened without the decision to signal. This implies that the causal chain of physiological events cannot give the whole story, since without the decision the causal chain would not have ended the way it did. I do not know how it is that decisions or intentions come to be transformed into bodily movements. Though an identity theory of mind and brain would no doubt see the problems very differently and thus provide an answer, I am not sure that we can know how intentions are translated into bodily movements; nor do I think we need to know or need to assume that it is possible or impossible to know for my view of reasons to be accepted.

We know how to move our arms. Someone can decide to move his arm, and putting that decision into effect is to move his arm. In order for him to move it certain events have to occur in his body of which he may have no knowledge. In general as agents we do not know how such events are triggered off except by our trying to do something. To say this may seem to imply the existence of more conscious acts—

whether of trying or volition—than actually occur. But we have to learn to do most actions and make corresponding bodily movements. While they are being learnt, we are trying to do something and not always succeeding. Once learnt we barely need to be aware of trying: we merely do the action. In most cases our bodies move in the way we want and intend.

I suggest that the relation between driving a car and the working of the car-engine is analogous to the relation between acting and the working of the body. In order to act I move my body, and this requires certain internal events in my body, while in order to drive the car, not only does Audrey have to press the accelerator, but also certain internal events in the engine must take place. There is no problem about the compatibility of a causal explanation of the car's moving forward in terms of the way the engine works with the explanation of it in terms of Audrey wanting to get from London to Birmingham. Each explanation is necessary to the full explanation of what is happening. In this case the characteristics to be explained, such as the driving from London to Birmingham, the ignition of a petrol and air mixture and the car moving are all connected, and the presence of each characteristic is necessary for the others. In other cases this may not be so, and the explanation of why what is happening has one characteristic is independent of the explanation of why what is happening also has another.

With actions and bodily movements the characteristics are connected. Just as the driver goes from London to Birmingham by the car moving from one place to the other, so the agent performs an action by means of certain bodily movements. What happens may be described in terms of the bodily movement or in terms of the action. If a complete explanation is attempted, then it has to include explanations related to each characteristic. Various explanatory factors would be mentioned, all of which would have to be present for the happening to occur. Completeness is impracticable and not usually wanted.

In the car-driving case we use a mechanical means to bring about a desired end; we initiate a causal chain which produces what we want, and that end-product can be said to constitute our action. It seems to me that bodily movements are of the same kind; we initiate a causal chain which results in the bodily movement which constitutes the action. In many such cases we are not aware of any gap; we do what we intend and thereby initiate the causal chain. Thus the characteristic of what happens which specifies the bodily movement is explained by means of that causal chain and by our intention in making that bodily movement. The characteristic of what happens which relates to its being an intentional action is explained by means of what is intended and one's reasons for so intending.

II—*The compatibility of causal explanations of actions with explanations by reasons*

A different problem of compatibility occurs if the possible explanations are of the same action. I have allowed that actions can be caused—in the narrow sense. Can an action which is explicable by reasons also be explained by causes? If so, how are the reasons and the causes related?

Consider again the example of the voter, Alice Miller. She is faced with choosing between the different candidates; she thinks about her choice and after deliberation decides to vote for Joan Scott. She has reasons for making the choice and it is a real choice. The way she votes is explained in terms of her reasons. However, it might rightly be argued that to say this is to look at the action in an individualistic way, isolating it from its context and limiting consideration of the action to one aspect of it. When she was considering the alternatives, the way she saw them and what she thought about them depended on the way her ideas and beliefs had developed within a particular social context. If the ways in which the alternatives are seen by the electorate and the actual patterns of voting are examined, then common patterns of deliberation and acting may be noticed which were not evident when her action was looked at on its own. A common language and thus a common conceptual system which has some deep-seated assumptions built into it may limit the ways in which she sees, describes or understands the situation. Furthermore there may be common beliefs or social habits which play a part in the way the situation is seen, whether these are common to the whole society or only to a group within it, membership of which is determined by a particular shared characteristic. If her environment had been different, if she had lived in a different social milieu, her way of considering the situation might have been different, and thus her choice—or what she saw her choice to be—would have been different. There having been such a difference does not require that she would have chosen one of the other alternatives; it only requires that she would have seen the alternative she chose differently. All these possibilities about the ways in which her deliberation and choice might have been affected do not need to take away her power of choice. She can be influenced by many factors—whether internal or external, whether consciously or unconsciously—and yet still have a choice for which she has reasons.

Let me try and elaborate on how this is possible. When an agent is determined to do an action it is an action of a particular sort. What is determined is that he does an action with one characteristic; but there may have been a number of possible actions which shared this characteristic. If so, the agent may choose any of them and yet still be determined in his action in the way already suggested. Given one description of the action it may be caused; given a different one it may have been chosen freely. An alcoholic's action in taking a drink may have been compulsive and thus not a matter of choice, but it would still be possible—and certainly not inconsistent—for him to have had a choice over what form of alcohol he took. If his action is described as one of taking an alcoholic drink, then it is caused; if his action is described as taking whisky rather than gin, then his action is freely chosen and he may have reasons for it. In this sense an action may be both determined by causes and freely chosen on the basis of reasons.

The account I have given of reasons in the context of deliberation makes it easy to show that this possibility involves no contradiction. For in deliberating we deliberate about alternatives, and there is no contradiction in supposing that the range and the nature of those alternatives is determined by factors outside our control, and that at the same time we choose between them on the basis of reasons. Thus even though a particular causal factor does not determine every aspect of an action, nevertheless if it had not had its effect on the agent the action might have been different in certain respects. Factors can determine the action we have chosen, while we still act on the basis of reasons, because the action may have a causal explanation under one description and an explanation by reasons under another.

This indicates, I think, that the possibility of explanations by reasons need not be inconsistent with the possibility of empirical enquiries and the formulation of testable generalisations about human beings. We can recognise that human actions have features of a kind which cannot be found in events which are the concern of the natural sciences, without ruling out the possibility of there being empirical generalisations about actions which hold for all people, for all people of a certain type or simply for one individual person through time. This is not to deny that there are difficulties about identifying correctly actions and their characteristics so that generalisations can be made about them.

III—*Explanations and responsibility*

In Chapter I I raised the problem of reconciling an agent's responsibility for his action with the possibility of its being explained. What has been said in this and earlier chapters now enables me to deal with the problem.

Frank Jones can stand his child crying no longer and hits her violently. A neighbour condemns his action as wicked and says that he ought to be severely punished, implying that he was responsible for what he did and could have acted otherwise. A social worker explains his action in terms of Frank's violent and disrupted childhood together with the social environment in which he lives—unemployment, cramped space and complaining neighbours. This explanation might seem to suggest that it was these factors which led to Frank hitting the child and, therefore, that he was not responsible for his action. Is it possible to reconcile the neighbour's point of view with the social worker's explanation or must they be contradictory?

If Frank's action is explained in terms of his reasons rather than in the social worker's way, then clearly no lack of responsibility is implied. If he acted for a reason then he evaluates his feature-wants or failed to do so when he could have. He could have evaluated differently and thus acted differently. If the agent could not have chosen other than he did, then he did not act for a reason.

The real problem here relates to causal explanations. There are various types of causal explanation consistent with responsibility, even when explanations by reasons are not included amongst those which are causal. The first type has already been mentioned in this chapter. Causal explanations may be correctly given of some characteristics of what is happening when an agent acts, while reasons may be given for others. The alcoholic's taking a drink may be caused, while his taking whisky rather than gin may be chosen; though not responsible for the former, he is for the latter. An agent may not be responsible for his accent but may be responsible for what he says. Thus an action can at the same time have a causal explanation and be responsible.

Similar explanations result from the way aspects of the context of the agent's decision-making are caused. The range of possibilities open to him may be limited, and these limits and the ways he sees the different alternatives may be given causal explanations. Thus Frank Jones's upbringing and social environment lead him to have certain feelings about his child and about the possible ways of dealing with her. These may be explained causally, but that they can be does not mean that he has no choice and cannot have reasons for what he does.

Another form of explanation was mentioned when his case was discussed in Chapter XI, Section II as an impulsive action. He had a reason for his action—he wanted the child to stop crying. Though he made no evaluation of his impulse-desire, he could have evaluated it and acted on his evaluation. There are difficulties about telling whether this is a correct account of the origination of his action; these will be mentioned in the next chapter and need not delay us here. If, then, he has a reason of this sort, it can nevertheless be said that his impulse-desire is a cause of his action in that it led to his action. This is consistent with his being responsible for the action, since he could have prevented the impulse-desire having its effect.

The extent of his responsibility may vary with the source of his failure to control his desire. On the one hand he may have failed because whatever he tried to do at the time, he could not have acted in any other way; nevertheless if in the past he had paid attention to his violent tendencies, he could have gradually established a habit of control. In such a case his responsibility is for not having made the required efforts in the past, just as the drunken driver may have responsibility for what he does when under the influence of drink because he could have stopped himself getting drunk. On the other hand he may have failed because he did not try at the time of his action, though he could have.

The circumstances in Frank Jones's case are not unlike those in which weakness of will is shown. The way the latter were dealt with in Chapter VII, Section II suggests yet another form of causal explanation compatible with responsibility. The strength and motivational force of impulse-desires can vary; as it increases, so does the evaluation of opposing feature-wants have to be higher if the impulse-desire is to be resisted. In a compulsive action the motivational force is so great that whatever evaluation the agent makes he cannot but act to satisfy the impulse-desire. Again there is a problem—to be discussed in the next chapter—in deciding whether the motivational force is so strong as to be compulsive or whether the agent could have controlled it. That the agent has an impulse-desire with a certain motivational force may be caused, and if he could control it but does not that desire may be said to cause his action. The degree of his responsibility will depend on the strength of the desire and how great his resistance to it has to be in order to overcome it.

I have suggested a number of ways in which causal explanations can be given for actions which the agent performs for reasons, and for which he is therefore responsible. These may not be the only ways, but they are sufficient to show that causal explanation does not automatically excuse the agent, though it may affect the degree to which he bears responsibility.

XIII
Verifiability

I—*Verification and covering-laws*

The discussion of compatibility indicated problems about how the strength of an impulse-desire can be estimated and about whether, if an agent attends to his impulse-desire, he can control it. Is it possible to justify the claim that Frank Jones could have controlled his? On what grounds do we say of an alcoholic that his drinking is compulsive, while of another drinker that his drinking is not? These questions are related to the more general question of how any explanation by reasons can be verified. How can we tell whether or not Dominic Joy and Michael Fitt (Chapter VIII, Section II) exercise because they want to reduce?

According to my account, reasons relate to the intention of the agent and, in the case of deliberative actions, to private processes of reasoning; none of these are directly accessible to an observer. This suggests that it is only the agent himself who can know what his reasons are and that an observer depends on the honesty and self-knowledge of the agent. However, there are cases—such as that of Geoffrey Washington (Chapter XI, Section IV)—in which an observer can with some assurance claim that an agent is mistaken about the explanation of his own action. The very concepts of rationalisation and self-deception presuppose this possibility. How, then, can an explanation by reasons be checked? The obstacles to finding objective ways of doing so are no doubt one reason for the popularity of the view that explanations of actions, like other explanations, should depend on empirically established generalisations. But such a view unduly limits the range of possible explanations and is likely to result in many actions either not being explicable at all or being explained inadequately. I shall argue that, though explanations in terms of reasons are not of a covering-law type and their conclusive verification may never be possible, nevertheless sufficient grounds can be given for accepting that particular explanations are correct and of the form I have suggested.

Beth Parker is trying to discover Norman Marriott's reasons for having sold his car. She knows that he has lost his job and concludes that he sold it because he wanted the money. Such an explanation is at first sight acceptable. On the basis of the information given it makes sense. The explanation makes his action reasonable because it shows that he does what other people would have done in his circumstances, especially when these are understood to include his wants. There seems to be an implicit reference to a generalisation. Certainly Beth's judgment of Norman's reasons is based on the application to his situation of her beliefs about how people generally respond in similar situations. Thus it looks as if the explanation is of a covering-law form. However, in the case of most explanations by reasons it is difficult—if not impossible—to find a covering-law with the universality required to deduce what is being explained. Rather such explanations are based on the way people tend to act or usually act.

It might be alleged that her explanation is adequate, though incomplete, because it is only what Hempel has called an explanation-sketch.[1] In theory, though not in practice, the full circumstances of Norman's situation—both what is happening to him and his own beliefs, wants and interests—together with generalisations about the ways people act would make it possible to deduce that Norman would sell his car. To explain Norman's action by his reasons, it is suggested, is to imply that there are covering-laws even if they can only be partially stated. The explanation is verified to the extent possible by testing the laws and checking that his circumstances are as stated.

Beth's explanation does not pretend to be complete because she has not got all the evidence required. She puts forward her explanation as sound because that is the way people tend to react and therefore there is good but not unchallengeable evidence for it. She neither claims nor is entitled to claim any more. Our rough and ready knowledge of people in general and of an individual's circumstances provides rough and ready explanations of why the individual acts the way he does. However, the reason for the way people in general react providing no more than partial evidence, is not the incompleteness of our knowledge. Even if such knowledge were complete and Norman's actions accorded with the way others would have acted, the correctness of the explanation would not be guaranteed, and his action would not be explained by the fact that others would have done the same. The fact that people have responded to a situation in one way does not mean that another agent must respond in the same way. To suppose he must would be to deny the essential element of choice in having reasons. Norman's evaluation is his own and not determined by any characteristics of his whether or not they are common to others as well. Any general statements which hold for most people most of the time are useful in providing a starting point for our understanding of other individuals and serve as one test, though in no way a conclusive one, for the correctness of what are alleged to be the agent's reasons. It is a sound practical principle that in many fundamental respects people of a common culture—and to a lesser degree from a common background—are alike, so that an agent's reasons are likely to be similar to those of another person from the same culture or the same background. Beth is right to start by using her knowledge of human nature and to base her judgment of Norman's reason on it. But her explanation may be wrong without any inadequacy in her knowledge. Norman may just evaluate differently from others. He may be short of money, but that may only be incidental to his decision. Rather he has come to think that cars pollute the atmosphere, and that though he still wants to be able to use a car for visiting friends and going shopping, he thinks that his wanting not to contribute to polluting the atmosphere is more important. Thus the factors he decides are to carry most weight are not the ones most others would think important. He may be eccentric, but it is nevertheless his reason.

The answer from the exponent of the covering-law is that though Norman is different from most, those differences are included in the statement of circumstances to which the explanatory law is to be applied. Thus anyone who feels strongly about not wanting to pollute the atmosphere sells their car and the explanatory force of his reason depends on this generalisation. But the fact that he has this want is not enough for it to constitute a reason, let alone a sufficient reason; he also has to evaluate it more highly than his other wants. If this element is also included in the generalisation, then it ceases to explain since it will be true by definition, stating that whatever want an agent evaluates most highly, he acts to satisfy. What explains his action is not the generalisation, but what is called the statement of his circumstances—that he evaluates this want more highly than his others.

An agent's reasons may seem inadequate or strange; the way he decides is his own way and he can act in a unique way or for reasons which he alone has. Those reasons may be criticised but cannot be denied him. Since agents determine their own reasons, we are not entitled to infer one person's reasons from those of another. Each person evaluates for himself; he may use the guidance of the evaluations of others, but he nevertheless decides on his own. Insofar as an explanation of an agent's action is by his reasons it makes no reference to anything outside himself. Nor does it make any essential reference to the way he has evaluated in the past. Each evaluation is open and undetermined by the reasons others have or by the agent's own reasons on other occasions. Therefore covering-laws either in terms of other people's actions or his own do not explain an action if it is performed for reasons.

II—Verification and evaluations
Beth starts to give an explanation in terms of what it would make sense for Norman's reasons to have been. But this is not sufficient for a correct explanation. Is she more likely to be successful if she relies on Norman's statement of his own reasons? Though this must count as strong evidence, he may

either not be telling the truth or be mistaken about his own reasons. His account of his reasons is less likely to be correct if, for instance, he has an ulterior motive for having, or for persuading an observer that he has, one reason rather than another. Various ways an agent can be wrong about his reasons have been discussed (Chapter XI, Section IV). However what an agent believes to be his reasons, subject to evidence to the contrary, would be rightly accepted as his real reasons.

Thus in searching for an agent's reasons we have a variety of information. We may have his report of what his reasons are. We may have evidence of the reasons which anyone would be expected to have when acting in the same way. We may have evidence of other actions of the agent, and what we know about him and influences on him independently of this situation. When all this evidence points to the same conclusion we have strong grounds for claiming that the explanation is the right one, though of course we may still be mistaken. Where the evidence conflicts, we may be able to discover more by making further enquiries. But if, when all the possible evidence has been assembled, there is still a conflict then we have to weigh the evidence on either side and reach a conclusion which, though still corrigible, can be supported by reasons.

Thus neither the agent nor the spectator of the action can ever be certain that they have the correct answer about the agent's reasons, or even that the action was the result of reasons. But this should not lead us to infer that we are not entitled to draw conclusions about reasons. We are entitled to do so; we have evidence for them, and can justify them. The evidence is of various different sorts, and it builds up a picture of the way an agent comes to act rather than pointing to any sort of a theory. There will be a much larger element of judgment involved and the tests for correctness will be less clear-cut, with little in the way of standard procedures being possible. It may, therefore, be more difficult to combat the charge of subjectivity, but it does not follow that there is no correct explanation or that all explanations are a matter of individual interpretation. Arguments and debate about the explanation to which the evidence points are possible, and like any conclusion to a piece of deliberation an explanation can be correct even though poorly supported, or incorrect though well supported.

III—*Verification and responsibility*

Related to the problem of verifying claims about reasons is the problem of verifying claims about responsibility. How can we tell whether an agent could have acted otherwise? How can we tell whether Frank Jones could have controlled his desire to hit his child? The question is whether the agent acts on reasons at all, and the answer takes much the same form as that to the question of what an agent's reasons are. We can support the claim that an agent is responsible with a variety of evidence, and the claim is justified by the evidence in favour being stronger than the evidence against.

We rightly start with the assumption that an agent is responsible unless there is evidence to the contrary. Such evidence may relate to the oddness of his action when compared either with the rest of his own actions or with those of others and more important may relate to the inconsistency of his action with the rest of his wants. Frank Jones's action and that of Agnes Brown, who is a kleptomaniac, in stealing a china ornament may be compared. Frank's action is not normal—most people are not so violent, nor is he usually so violent. Moreover, hitting the child is clearly against his own interests and incompatible with much else that he wants; he has shown love for the child and does not want it to suffer, nor does he want the shame and punishment which are likely to follow. It is difficult to see how he could have decided to do what he did and failed to attend to his opposing wants. Agnes's action is also overwhelmingly against her own interests. She neither needs nor wants the ornament and is well enough off to buy it if she did. She knows she will be punished, though that means little to her at the time. On other occasions she has a strong moral sense. The reasons against her action are so strong and so obvious that it is difficult to see how she could have failed to pay attention to them, if she had in any way made a decision. Though there are similarities with Frank's case, there is a difference in that his action does satisfy a clear and conscious want while it is difficult to find any want which Agnes could consciously have. Therefore, on these grounds, Frank's action is more likely to be under his control than is Agnes's.

Further arguments may be given for and against Frank having been able to control his want. Other people control their actions in such circumstances, so why cannot he? Is he suffering from mental illness? Or are the pressures on him so much greater than those which other people are subjected to in similar situations? Would it have had any effect on his action if he had evaluated differently? As in the verification of reasons, so—not only in Frank's case but more generally—reasons for and against the agent being responsible and being able to control his action have to be weighed against each other and a conclusion is reached on the basis of those evaluations. There are no simple tests for verifying whether or not an agent has acted on reasons or for what those reasons are. But claims can be supported and challenged, and hence the correctness of attributing reasons is a proper matter for rational debate.

XIV
Conclusion

Most accounts of explanation examine and analyse the explanations themselves. They take a correct explanation of an action and look at the relation between what is mentioned in the explanation and the action which is explained. Such accounts are essentially backward looking, considering only actions which have occurred. This is the wrong approach: we can only understand the way explanations function by looking at the ways in which actions come to be performed. To explain an action is to give an account of the factors which led to the action taking place and their relation to the action they explain. In a deliberative action the agent decides on his action as a result of his deliberations, and to understand why he acted in the way he did we must examine the way he deliberated. Therefore an account of the explanation of such actions must include an account of deliberation. My account rejected the view that any deliberation, if adequate, must be reducible to logical reasoning, or that its structure must essentially be logical. The errors resulting from such a view occur widely, not only in discussions of deliberation or practical reasoning, but also in the philosophy of science, for instance in the way empirical hypotheses are arrived at and supported, and in moral philosophy. My account of deliberation points to the need for broader concepts of reasoning and for greater appreciation of the importance of judgment, needs which have wide educational implications and deserve much more attention.

In deliberation an agent considers which factors are relevant to making a decision; he evaluates those which are relevant and thus decides which are to constitute reasons for and reasons against different conclusions; finally he assesses and evaluates the reasons in relation to each other so as to reach the final conclusion. The reasons in favour of what he decides are thus determined in the process of the deliberation. An agent's reasons may be expressed by reference to his wants. To say that a certain want is an agent's reason is to say something about the agent's evaluation of his want, and is not to say that the want is a cause of the action. The want can only produce the action if the agent makes the want into a reason, and into a sufficiently important reason, for him to act on it. The only exception to this is when the want directly produces the action irrespective of the agent's evaluation of it. In this case the want does not provide the agent's reason but causes the action. This gives one ground for refusing to say that the reason for an action is its cause.

To say that reasons are not causes is not to deny that causal factors may affect an action which is explained by reasons, and can do so without making choice impossible. In acting on reasons an agent evaluates the factors he takes to be relevant and decides what are to be his reasons. But the way he sees the action and the alternatives from which he chooses may be subject to causal influences, as may the way he understands the factors he is evaluating. Some part of the context within which he makes his choice may be determined, and causal explanations may be given for it. Such explanations could be, and almost certainly would be, relevant to an understanding of the action, and would in no way be incompatible with the action being chosen, an action for which the agent is responsible and for which reasons are given. To explain an action fully we not only need to understand the agent's reasons and how he arrived at them, but also the way all other factors affected his awareness of and response to the situation in which he acted.

Insofar as an agent acts on reasons he is responsible; if his reasons do not determine or could not have determined his action then he is not responsible for it. Hence it seems as if there is a clear-cut division between the actions for which the agent is responsible and those for which he is not. But the same action may be given a purely causal explanation under one description and an explanation by reasons under another. An agent may have no choice about doing an action with a particular characteristic, while he may be able to choose among the range of actions which share this characteristic. He is not responsible in this case for doing an action with that characteristic, while he is responsible for whatever choice he makes within the range of possibilities. The extent of an agent's responsibility may be assessed by considering the descriptions under which the action is caused and the descriptions under which it is based on reasons. Some descriptions may not be central to our interests in assessing responsibility. Thus the fact that an agent is seeking power— under which description his action might be caused—may be relatively unimportant compared with whether he did so at the expense of others or for their benefit.

In assessing responsibility it is preferable not to state the problem wholly in terms of alternative descriptions. Rather it may be assessed in terms of the extent to which the range of alternatives open to the agent when he acts is limited, and in terms of the ways in which he sees those alternatives and in which each affects him. To do this it is necessary to ascertain all the causal factors which influence him when he decides to act. If the assessment of responsibility is in the context of law-breaking, then it is not sufficient to look only at the action itself. It is also necessary to look at the way the agent comes to the decision to act illegally and the background to that decision. The degree of responsibility does not depend on the kind of action it is, but on the agent's individual decision-making process—or in some cases on the lack of such a process.

We can give an explanation of someone's action, and thus come to an understanding of it, without suggesting that his responsibility is in any way diminished. Insofar as his reasons are given we understand how the agent came to his decision to act in this way, and this is quite different from ascertaining the factors which might have made him act in the way he did. Because of the evaluative content of reasons the explanation does not provide us with information which could have been obtained in advance and which, if it had been, would have enabled us to predict the action. In the case of actions explanation and prediction are not closely connected.

Thus the very fact that an explanation of a criminal's—or

anyone else's—action can be given is not in itself sufficient to diminish responsibility. In a particular case it may be difficult to assess the degree of responsibility because of the lack of impartial evidence about the alleged criminal's thinking, especially as he has a strong motive for persuading the court that he was not responsible for what he did. It is indeed impossible to know with certainty whether an agent could have acted differently or what the extent of his choice was. However, it is still possible to support a conclusion about responsibility with evidence. Our understanding of the way an agent came to decide on his action and the background to his decision may be fallible, but it can be defended and used as a basis for a claim about the agent's responsibility. In spite of this it is still arguable the extent to which a legal system should take into account the degree of responsibility of a criminal and in what range of cases it should do so.

My account has shown that the importance of psychological and sociological factors is not ruled out by explanations in terms of reasons which involve freedom of choice. Moreover I think it can be shown that it allows, even requires, the possibility of a variety of approaches within the social sciences. Arguments about, for instance, the one correct method in sociology are misguided. Clearly the positivist approach makes assumptions which, if it were the only possible approach, would limit the range of sociological explanations which can be given. There may be empirical generalisations based on observations about what happens within a society, and these may reveal factors which affect the way an agent understands his situation and decides between alternatives; but such explanations must leave out much that is important. Other alternatives such as participant observation, which place more emphasis on the individual's point of view, may also provide material for explanations, though how far such approaches can generalise and test their claims is not clear. But whatever view is taken of the nature of sociological and psychological explanations, if such an explanation only relates to determining factors—whether psychological or sociological—and if the action being explained is performed for a reason, then the explanation cannot be complete since it cannot take account of the agent's evaluation.

What I have said about reasons attempts to provide a philosophical account of the explanation of actions which is consistent with a humanistic and non-determinist view of man, and yet allows that a great variety of empirical investigations may help us in the understanding of human actions. I have two main purposes in developing this account of reasons: firstly, to reconcile the possibility of free-will with the possibility of understanding and explaining actions; secondly, to provide a philosophical basis for an understanding of actions in which the use of the widest range of resources is possible, and more particularly to provide a basis for the claim that there is no one correct method for the empirical study of human action, but that very different methods are needed and are indeed compatible. I hope that what I have said goes some way to fulfilling these purposes.

Notes

Preface
1. R. Edgley, *Reason in Theory and Practice* (London, 1969).
2. 'Reasons as Explanations', *Mind*, Vol. 83 (1974), pp. 180–93.
3. See, especially, J. Macmurray, *The Self as Agent* (London, 1957) and *Persons in Relation* (London, 1961).

Chapter I
1. For a defence of this point, see my paper, 'Philosophy and the Social Sciences', *Proceedings of the Aristotelian Society*, Vol. 69 (1968–9), pp. 51–72.
2. The most important discussion of this is in Edgley, *Reason in Theory and Practice*.

Chapter II
1. David Hume, *A Treatise of Human Nature*, edited by L. A. Selby-Bigge (Oxford, 1888), Book II, Part III, Section III, p. 413.
2. Hume, Book III, Part I, Section I, p. 463.
3. Hume, Book III, Part I, Section I, p. 458.
4. K. R. Popper, *The Logic of Scientific Discovery* (London, 1959), p. 31.
5. N. R. Hanson, 'The Logic of Discovery', *Journal of Philosophy*, Vol. 55 (1958), pp. 1073–89; *Patterns of Discovery* (Cambridge, 1958); and 'Notes towards a Logic of Discovery', in R. J. Bernstein, ed., *Perspectives on Peirce* (New Haven, 1965), pp. 42–65.
6. P. Alexander, 'On the Logic of Discovery', *Ratio*, Vol. 7 (1965), pp. 219–32.

Chapter III
1. For a survey of the response to what he calls the 'phenomenological' account of wants, see W. Alston, 'Motives and Motivation', in P. Edwards, ed., *The Encyclopaedia of Philosophy* (New York, 1967), Vol. 5, pp. 399–409. For a general discussion, see also J. C. B. Gosling, *Pleasure and Desire* (Oxford, 1969).
2. See P. H. Nowell-Smith, *Ethics* (Harmondsworth, 1954).
3. G. E. M. Anscombe, *Intention* (Oxford, 1957), p. 67.

Chapter IV
1. Hume, *Treatise*, Book II, Part I, Section I, p. 275.
2. Hume, *Treatise*, Book III, Part I, Section I, p. 458.
3. P. S. Ardal, *Passion and Value in Hume's Treatise* (Edinburgh, 1966), p. 94.
4. Hume, *Treatise*, Book II, Part III, Section III, p. 417.
5. Hume, *Treatise*, Book II, Part III, Section IV, p. 419.

Chapter V
1. See S. F. Barker, 'Must Every Inference be either Deductive or Inductive?' in M. Black, ed., *Philosophy in America* (London, 1965), pp. 58–73.
2. R. M. Hare, *The Language of Morals* (Oxford, 1952).
3. A. J. P. Kenny, 'Practical Inference,' *Analysis*, Vol. 26 (1965–6), pp. 65–75, and *Will, Freedom and Power* (Oxford, 1975), Chapter 5.
4. As well as Kenny, see also G. E. M. Anscombe, *Intention*, and 'Thought and Action in Aristotle' in R. Bambrough, ed., *New Essays on Plato and Aristotle* (London, 1965), pp. 143–58; M. Mothersill, 'Anscombe's Account of the Practical Syllogism', *Philosophical Review*, Vol. 71 (1962), pp. 448–61; G. H. von Wright, *Explanation and Understanding* (London, 1971) and 'On So-called Practical Inference', *Acta Sociologica*, Vol. 15 (1969), pp. 39–53.
5. See J. Dewey, *The Quest for Certainty* (London, 1930).
6. For a related discussion which takes a rather different view, see K. Graham, 'Belief and the Limits of Irrationality', *Inquiry*, Vol. 17 (1974), pp. 315–26.
7. For discussions of decision theory, see W. Edwards and A. Tversky, ed., *Decision Making* (Harmondsworth, 1967); R. J. Audley *et al*, *Decision Making* (London, 1967).
8. Hare, *The Language of Morals*.
9. See references in footnote 4 above; and G. H. von Wright, *An Essay in Deontic Logic and the General Theory of Action* (Amsterdam, 1968).
10. Kenny, 'Practical Inference' and *Will, Freedom and Power*.
11. Kenny, *Will, Freedom and Power*, p. 39.
12. Kenny, *Will, Freedom and Power*, p. 85.
13. Kenny, *Will, Freedom and Power*, p. 95.

Chapter VI
1. G. E. M. Baier 'Good Reasons', *Philosophical Studies* Vol. 4 (1953), pp. 1–15; G. E. M. Baier, *The Moral Point of View* (Ithaca, 1958); S. Toulmin, *The Place of Reason in Ethics* (Cambridge, 1950); S. Toulmin, *The Uses of Argument* (Cambridge, 1958); K. Nielsen, 'The "Good Reasons Approach" and "Ontological Justifications" of Morality', *Philosophical Quarterly*, Vol. 9 (1959), pp. 116–30; K. Nielsen, 'Appealing to Reason', *Inquiry*, Vol. 5 (1962), pp. 65–84.

2. For relevant discussions, see: M. A. Boden, *Artificial Intelligence and Natural Man* (Hassocks, Sussex, 1977); A. I. Sloman, *The Computer Revolution in Philosophy* (Hassocks, Sussex, 1978).
3. See R. W. Hepburn and I. Murdoch, Symposium: 'Vision and Choice in Morality', *Proceedings of the Aristotelian Society*, Supplementary Vol. 30 (1956), pp. 14–58; N. Cooper and R. Edgley, Symposium, 'Rules and Morality', *Proceedings of the Aristotelian Society*, Supplementary Vol. 33 (1959), pp. 159–94.
4. J. Habermas, *Knowledge and Human Interests*, translated by J. J. Shapiro (London, 1972).

Chapter VII
1. R. Edgley, *Reason in Theory and Practice*.
2. M. Bratman, 'Practical Reasoning and Weakness of the Will', *Noûs*, Vol. 13 (1979), pp. 153–71, discusses weakness of will in these terms.
3. See A. Harrison, *Making and Thinking* (Hassocks, Sussex, 1978).
4. See also D. Davidson, 'How is Weakness of the Will Possible?' in J. Feinberg, ed., *Moral Concepts* (London, 1969), pp. 93–113; G. W. Mortimore, ed., *Weakness of Will* (London, 1971).

Chapter VIII
1. D. Davidson, 'Actions, Reasons and Causes', *Journal of Philosophy*, Vol. 60 (1963), pp. 685–700. This has been reprinted in A. R. White, ed., *The Philosophy of Action* (London, 1968), pp. 79–94. Page references will be given to both; the bracketed reference is to White.
2. Davidson, 'Actions, Reasons and Causes', p. 685 (p. 79).
3. Davidson, 'Actions, Reasons and Causes', p. 686 (pp. 79–80).
4. See A. I. Melden, *Free Action* (London, 1961) and my discussion of it in the next chapter.
5. Davidson, 'Actions, Reasons and Causes', p. 687 (p. 81).
6. Davidson, 'Actions, Reasons and Causes', p. 693 (p. 87).
7. I. Kant, *Groundwork of the Metaphysic of Morals*, translated by H. J. Paton, as *The Moral Law* (London, 1948), pp. 67–8.
8. H. J. Paton, *The Categorical Imperative* (London, 1947), pp. 60–1.
9. Hare, *The Language of Morals*, p. 56.
10. Hare, *The Language of Morals*, pp. 58–9.
11. Hare, *The Language of Morals*, p. 59.
12. For a valuable discussion of Hare's views, see R. W. Beardsmore, *Moral Reasoning* (London, 1969), Chapter I.
13. J. D. Mabbott; 'Moral Rules', *The Proceedings of the British Academy*, Vol. XXXIX (1953), p. 97.
14. For the distinction between universal and general, see R. M. Hare, 'Principles', *Proceedings of the Aristotelian Society*, Vol. LXXIII (1972–3), pp. 2–4.
15. See J. P. Sartre, *Existentialism and Humanism*, translated by P. Mairet, (London, 1948).

Chapter IX
1. Davidson, 'Actions, Reasons and Causes'; W. Alston 'Wants, Actions and Causal Explanations' in H. N. Castaneda, ed., *Minds, Intentionality and Perception* (Detroit, 1967), pp. 301–56; A. I. Goldman, *A Theory of Human Action* (Englewood Cliffs, 1970), Chapter 4.
2. Melden, *Free Action*, p. 88.
3. Melden, *Free Action*, p. 114.
4. Melden, *Free Action*, p. 157.
5. Melden, *Free Action*, p. 109.
6. Melden, *Free Action*, especially pp. 100–103.
7. Melden, *Free Action*, p. 102.
8. For an admirable discussion of some of the difficulties of the logical connection argument, including some of those I have mentioned, see D. Locke, 'Reasons, Wants and Causes', *American Philosophical Quarterly*, Vol. 11 (1974), pp. 169–79.
9. Melden, *Free Action*, p. 113.
10. Melden, *Free Action*, p. 88.

Chapter X
1. Hume, *A Treatise of Human Nature*.
2. R. B. Braithwaite, *Scientific Explanation* (Cambridge, 1953).
3. A. I. Melden, 'Desires as Causes of Actions' in F. C. Dommeyer, ed., *Current Philosophical Issues* (Springfield, 1966).
4. J. L. Mackie, 'Causes and Conditions', *American Philosophical Quarterly*, Vol. 2 (1965), p. 245.
5. *E.g.*, P. Alexander, 'Are Causal Laws Purely General?', *Proceedings of the Aristotelian Society*, Supplementary Vol. 44 (1970), pp. 15–36.
6. D. Davidson, 'Freedom to Act', in T. Honderich, ed., *Essays on Freedom of Action* (London, 1973), p. 153.
7. Davidson, 'Freedom to Act', pp. 153–4.
8. A. I. Goldman, *A Theory of Human Action*, Ch. 4.
9. By K. Graham in a comment on a draft of this book. I am indebted to him.

Chapter XI
1. S. Freud, *New Introductory Lectures on Psychoanalysis*, tr. by J. Strachey, Pelican Freud Library, Vol. 2 (Harmondsworth, 1973), p. 103.
2. For a helpful discussion of unconscious reasons, and indeed of important aspects of all explanation by reasons, see P. Alexander, 'Rational Behaviour and Psycho-analytic Explanation', *Mind*, Vol. 71 (1962), pp. 326–41. It is discussed in T. Mischel, 'Concerning Rational Behaviour and Psycho-analytic Explanations', *Mind*, Vol. 74 (1965), pp. 71–8, and J. Balmuth 'Psycho-analytic Explanation', *Ibid.*, pp. 229–35, to both of which Alexander responded in 'Psychoanalysis

Notes

and the Explanation of Behaviour', *Mind*, Vol. 80 (1971), pp. 391–402. See also H. Mullane, 'Psychoanalytic Explanation and Rationality', *Journal of Philosophy*, Vol. 68 (1971), pp. 413–26.

3. See H. Fingarette, *Self-Deception* (London, 1969) and P. L. Gardiner, Error, Faith and Self-Deception', *Proceedings of the Aristotelian Society*, Vol. 70 (1969–70), pp. 221–43.
4. For a discussion of the rôle of habits in this type of explanation see J. Macmurray, *The Boundaries of Science* (London, 1939).
5. S. Freud, 'Analysis of a Phobia in a Five-year-old Boy', *Case Histories I*, Pelican Freud Library, Vol. 8 (Harmondsworth, 1977), pp. 169–305. See H. Mullane's discussion of the case in 'Unconscious Cleverness—The Unconscious Ego' *Scientia*, Vol. 7 (1966), pp. 1–10. He gives an argument for the interpretation of the evidence which I find wholly convincing, though I do not accept some of the conclusions he draws. See also R. Brown, *Social Psychology* (New York, 1965), pp. 352–74.
6. See Mullane, 'Unconscious Cleverness—The Unconscious Ego'.
7. Freud, *Case Histories I*, p. 284.

Chapter XII
1. Kant, Groundwork of the Metaphysic of Morals, p. 119.
2. G. Ryle, *The Concept of Mind* (London, 1949), p. 19.
3. Melden, *Free Action*, pp. 73ff.
4. See Goldman, *A Theory of Human Action*; Davidson, 'Actions, Reasons and Causes'; and Anscombe, *Intention*.

Chapter XIII
1. C. G. Hempel, 'The Function of General Laws in History', *Journal of Philosophy*, Vol. 39 (1942), pp. 35–48.

Summary of the Main Examples

Chapter I
Non-accidental injuries to children　　　　　　　　　　1f
　　See also Ch. XI, pp. 147f; Ch. XII, pp. 167–9;
　　　Ch. XIII, pp. 171, 176f.

Chapter II
Thomas Fagg considers whether to give up smoking　　13–16
　　See also Ch. VI, pp. 89f; Ch. VIII, pp. 105f.
A car fails to start　　　　　　　　　　　　　　　　　14
George Green tries to decide whether to plant out his
tomatoes　　　　　　　　　　　　　　　　　　　　　20

Chapter III
Jane Smith crosses the road　　　　　　　　　　　　25, 29f
Helen looks in a shop-window　　　　　　　　　　　28
Joseph Appleby plays the trumpet to the dislike of
Mrs. Grump　　　　　　　　　　　　　　　　　　　32
　　See also Ch. VIII, pp. 116–19.

Chapter IV
Matthew Dyer wants to see the Taj-Mahal　　　　　　36–44

Chapter V
Choosing the best route from London to Cambridge　　48
Adrian Flower wants to prevent the building of a
new road　　　　　　　　　　　　　　　　　　　　50–4
An engineer works out how to bridge a river　　　　　51f
Choosing a house with a garden　　　　　　　　　　52f
Ann Elworthy decides whether or not to try to go to the
University　　　　　　　　　　　　　　　　　　　　54f
Medicine is a good career for John　　　　　　　　　57f, 60
Angela Williams and Kenneth Carter decide whether a
mentally handicapped child should be admitted to an
institution　　　　　　　　　　　　　　　　　　　　64f
Gerald Austin tries to make up his mind about how to
acquire a car　　　　　　　　　　　　　　　　　　　66f

Summary of the Main Examples

Chapter VI
Antony Arbuckle gives advice about driving from A to B	77f, 81
Robert Sturmer and Donald Cox compare the productiveness of two varieties of apple tree	80
Mary Casson advises Kevin Granger on the choice of a career	84–8
Thomas Fagg considers whether to give up smoking See also Ch. II, pp. 13–16; Ch. VIII, pp. 105f.	89f

Chapter VII
Jack and Jill consider adopting Jeremy and Joanna	94–7
Arthur Brown decides how to punish Gordon Smart	98–102
Peter Paine is due for a check-up at the dentist	101

Chapter VIII
Thomas Fagg considers whether to give up smoking See also Ch. II, pp. 13–16; Ch. VI, pp. 89f.	105f
Why the short-cut was not taken	106
Rachel considers whether to have an abortion	108
Michael Fitt and Dominic Joy want to reduce and exercise See also Ch. XIII, p. 171.	110–12
Eileen Bird also wants to lose weight	111f
Joseph Appleby plays the trumpet to the dislike of Mrs. Grump See also Ch. III, p. 32.	116–19

Chapter IX
Melden's car driver raises his arm and signals	123, 129
Explaining the mending of a fuse	125
Snoles and catholes	126f
Rebecca stands up	126f
Bernard Bissett raises his arm and signals See also Ch. XII, pp. 160–3.	129f

Chapter X
Sam Buchanan and Victoria Adams are told by a hypnotist to open the window	134–7
Margaret Johnson is an alcoholic and wants a drink	136–8
Len Bateman is a social drinker and wants a drink	136–8
Davidson's climber loosens his grip on the rope	138f, 141f
Bridget Macdonald, while driving, sees someone collapse	140

Summary of the Main Examples

Chapter XI

Barbara Simmons brakes hard and frightens her passenger	145–7
Frank Jones hits his child violently	147f
See also Ch. I, pp. 1f; Ch. XII, pp. 167–9; Ch. XIII, pp. 171, 176f.	
William winds his watch whenever he takes it off	148–50
Philip, when questioned, puts his arms behind his back	148f
Basil is habitually rude to women he dislikes	148f
Carol Chatterton tries to guard her tongue	151f
Derek scratches his ear when he sees a dog	152f
Colin has a speech mannerism	152f
Geoffrey Washington tells Mrs. Smith that her hat doesn't suit her	154–6
See also Ch. XIII, p. 171	
Freud's case of Little Hans	157f

Chapter XII

Bernard Bissett raises his arm and signals	160–3
See also Ch. IX, pp. 129f.	
Alice Miller votes in an election	161f, 165f
Audrey wants to get from London to Birmingham	162, 164
Frank Jones hits his child violently	167–9
See also Ch. I, pp. 1f; Ch. XI, pp. 147f; Ch. XIII, pp. 171, 176f.	

Chapter XIII

Frank Jones hits his child violently	171, 176f
See also Ch. I, pp. 1f; Ch. XI, pp. 147f; Ch. XII, pp. 167–9.	
Michael Fitt and Dominic Joy want to reduce and exercise	171
See also Ch. VIII, pp. 110–12	
Geoffrey Washington tells Mrs. Smith that her hat doesn't suit her	171
See also Ch. XI, pp. 154–6.	
Beth Parker tries to discover why Norman Marriott has sold his car	172–5
Agnes Brown is a kleptomaniac	176f

Index

Actions
  characteristics of, 25, 30, 117,
    120, 129, 130, 166
  compulsive, 103, 110, 113, 153,
    155
  context of, 159, 161, 165, 168
  deliberative, 6, 110, 128
  description of, 24, 128, 130,
    160, 166
  immediate, 6, 38, 130–1, 144ff
  individuation of, 30
  non-deliberative, 10, 143
  origination of, 3, 4, 6, 159
Action-guiding, 31, 108
Alcoholics and alcoholism, 29,
    136, 166, 168, 171
Alexander, P., 19, 183, 186
Alston, W., 183, 186
Anscombe, G. E. M., 31, 183–4
Ardal, P. S., 40, 184
Attitudes, 111, 129
Audley, R. J., 184

Baier, G. E. M., 74, 184
Balmuth, J., 186
Barker, S. F., 184
Beardsmore, R. W., 185
Beliefs, 107, 138
Boden, M. A., 185
Bodily movements, 134, 159–65
Brain-impulses, 163
Braithwaite, R. B., 133, 186
Bratman, M., 185
Brown, R., 187

Causal chains, 165
  explanation, 159, 168
  relations, 124, 133

Causality, 5, 9, 41–2, 107,
    113–14, 123, Ch. X passim
  the regularity view of, 124
Central and non-central cases, 23,
    33
Changing one's mind, 119
Choice, 2, 4, 7, 16, 24, 29, 42, 49,
    63, 65, 91, 115, 166, 173
Commitment, 56, 61–2
Comparing and comparisons,
    75–89
Computers, 79
Conditioning, 156
Consciousness, 22, 33, 41
Cooper, N., 185
Covering-laws, 171–4
Creativity, 18

Davidson, D., 108–10, 112–14,
    129, 138, 141, 185–7
Decision, 9, 94, 99, 116
Decision-making, 14, 45, 48–9, 51,
    64, 68, 71, 75, 84, 89, 91, 127
Decision-theory, 54, 68
Deduction, 6, 14, 18–19, 47, 52,
    55, 58–62, 66, 71, 73, 79,
    85–6
Deductivist view, 70–1, 75, 86
Deliberation, 6–8, 11, 16, 22, 43,
    47, 73, 105, 128
  alternative account of, 74
  Humean view of, 7–8, 10–12,
    14–17, 19, 22, 48, 54–5, 63,
    69, 73
  practical and theoretical, 92, 94,
    98
  real structure of, 59
  structure of actual, 15, 56

Index

Desires (see also Wants), 9, 12, 15, Ch. III *passim*, 34, 124, 138
 compulsive, 37, 46, 69, 136
 strength of, 16, 36, 43–4, 69, 155, 169
Dewey, J., 184
Discovery, 18–19
Dispositions, 149

Edgley, R., x, 98, 183, 185
Edwards, W., 184
Evaluation, 6, 9, 37, 44–5, 64–5, 75–6, 80, 86, 89–93, 95, 103, 107, 111–12, 114, 131, 137, 139–41, 147, 168–9, 173–4
Existentialism, 120
Explanations, 28, 30, Ch. VIII *passim*
 compatibility of, 2, 4, 10, Ch. XII *passim*
 psychological, 160
 sociological, 160
Explanation-sketch, 171

Feature-wants, 7–8, 23–8, 30–3, , Ch. IV *passim*, 36, 45, 89, 92–3, 95, 97, 105–9, 111–13, 117, 120, 129, 131, 136–7, 169
 as causes, 45–6, 70
 causes of, 45–6
 conditions for, 26–33, 37, 42, 45
 deliberative, 118
 evaluation of, 45, 97
Feelings, 15, 34, 39
 introspectible, 38
 strength of, 39–40, 44, 68
Fingarette, H., 187
Freud, S., 143, 157–8, 186–7

Gardiner, P. L., 187
Generalisations, 21, 167, 171ff
 and reasons, 120
Goldman, A. I., 138, 186–7
Gosling, J. C. B., 183

Graham, K., 184, 186

Habermas, J., 88, 185
Habits, 143, 148–53, 157–8, 169
 deliberation and formation of, 150
Hanson, N. R., 19, 183
Hare, R. M., 47, 69, 114, 116, 118–19, 184–5
Harrison, A., 185
Hempel, C. G., 172, 187
Hepburn, R. W., 185
Hume, D., 7, 11–12, 22, 34, 40–1, 132, 183–4, 187
Humean-desires, 34ff, 42, 44
 conditions for, 35, 41
Hypnosis, 112, 134–5
Hypotheses, formation of, 17, 19
Hypothetico-deductive method, 17

Identity theory, 163
Imagination, 101
Impressions, 7, 34, 39–40, 128
Impulse-desires, 7, 36, 39, 43, 46, 95–6, 102–3, 118, 147, 155, 168–9, 171
Induction, 17, 19, 47
Inference, 19, 48
Infinite regress, 139
Intention, 128–32, 146–7, 161
Introspection, 33, 35, 37–8, 40–1
INUS conditions, 133, 135

Judgment, 75, 78, 84, 147
Justification, 5, 56, 59, 146

Kant, I., 114–15, 119, 160, 185 187
Kenny, A. J. P., 47, 70–1, 184

Liking, 31
Locke, D., 186
Logic, 6, 47, 59, 65, 69, 75, 88
Logical connection argument, 108, Ch. IX *passim*, 141–2

Mabbott, J. D., 115, 185

Mackie, J. L., 133, 186
Macmurray, J., xi, 183, 187
Maxims, 114
Melden, A. I., 108, 123-5, 127-8, 129-30, 132, 160, 185-7
Mischel, T., 186
Mistakes, 63-4, 112-13
Moral judgments, 59, 115
  principles, 59-60, 84
Morality, 44, 114
Mothersill, M., 184
Motivation, 32, 96, 102, 123, 160, 169
Mullane, H., 187
Murdoch, I., 185

Negligence, 151-2
Nielsen, K., 184
Norms, 120
Noumenal world, 160
Nowell-Smith, P. H., 183

Objective standards, 86-7
Ordinary language, 23

Passions, 12-14, 34
  calm and violent, 40-1
Paton, H. J., 114, 185
Peirce, C. S., 19
Phobias, 157
Popper, K. R., 17-18, 183
Preferences, 28, 54, 68
  formation of, 54
Premisses, suppressed, 56-8, 60
Pro-attitudes, 27, 29, 31-2, 40, 44-5, 108-9, 156
Psychological factors, 181
Purposes, 48-9, 51-2, 152

Rationalisations, 113
Reasoning, 5, 16, 42, 69
  actual, 53, 56
  factual, 14, 17
  logical, 65-7
  logical structure of, 53, 56
  non-deductive, 8, 86
  principles of, 99

real structure of, 56, 62
standards of, 74
Reasons, 3, 9, 28, 59, 81, 85-8, 90-1, Ch. VIII *passim*, 146
  and causes, 3-5, 9, 107, 123, Ch. X *passim*
  good, 74-5, 86, 92
  prima facie, 90, 109-14, 122, 130, 139
  primary, 108-9, 112
  unconscious, 143-4, 153ff
Redescription, 126-7, 129
Reduction of deliberation to logical reasoning, 15, 60, 73, 77, 81
Re-evaluation, 131
Response feature, 150
Responsibility, 2, 4, 10, 65, 167-70, 176, 179-80
Retroduction, 19
Rules, 78, 80, 114ff
Ryle, G., 187

Sartre, J-P., 121, 185
Satisfactoriness, 70-1
Self-deception, 101, 154, 171
Sensations, 34-5
Sloman, A. I., 185
Social sciences, 10, 181
Sociological factors, 181
Stimulus-feature, 150
Syllogism, practical, 12, 14-15, 50, 65, 71, 115

Toulmin, S., 184
Trying, 31, 164
Tversky, A., 184

Values, 15, 42
Verification, 10, Ch. XIII *passim*
Volition, 164
Voluntary and involuntary, 28-9, 104, 110, 133, 138

Wants (see also Desires), 7, Ch. III *passim*, 34-5, 52
  choosing one's, 43, 63
  competing, 96

compulsive, 23
conflicts of, 8, 15–16, 43, 45, 65, 70, 156
control of, 176
dispositional, 23–6
Humean view of, 23–4, 33, 38, 41–3
under-determination of, 52–3

Weakness of the will, 98, 100–1, 103, 155, 169
Weighing up factors, 99–100
reasons, 155
What-explanations, 125–7, 131
Why-explanations, 125–7, 131, 142
Wishing, 27
von Wright, G. H., 69, 184